THE ULTIMATE CAVAPOO GUIDE

From Puppyhood to Senior Years-
Training, Nutrition, Health, and
Responsible Ownership

CHARLES E. GABRIEL

Contents

Chapter 1

Introduction

Dogs have long held a cherished place in human lives, serving as companions, protectors, and emotional anchors. Among the diverse world of canine companions, the Cavapoo has emerged as one of the most sought-after breeds, captivating hearts with its blend of beauty, intelligence, and gentle temperament. For prospective pet owners seeking a loving, adaptable, and emotionally intuitive dog, the Cavapoo offers an ideal balance of traits that satisfy the needs of families, seniors, and those looking for therapy or emotional support animals. This chapter serves as the opening gateway to understanding the Cavapoo, setting the stage for responsible ownership, and outlining the purpose of this comprehensive guide.

The Rising Popularity of the Cavapoo

Over the past two decades, Cavapoos have experienced a remarkable surge in popularity worldwide. Their appeal lies not only in their appearance but also in the unique combination of traits inherited from their parent breeds—the Cavalier King Charles Spaniel and the Poodle. This hybrid has become a symbol of modern companion dogs, representing a shift in dog ownership trends toward smaller, more adaptable, and highly social breeds.

Several factors contribute to the Cavapoo's increasing popularity. First, their size makes them ideal for a variety of living situations, from spacious homes with backyards to urban apartments. Their small-to-medium stature allows them to comfortably fit into a household without overwhelming space or requiring extensive physical activity. Secondly, the Cavapoo's intelligence and trainability appeal to owners seeking a dog that can integrate seamlessly into family life and daily routines. Unlike some breeds that may require specialized handling, Cavapoos typically respond well to positive reinforcement methods, making them approachable for both first-time and experienced dog owners.

Moreover, the breed's emotional intelligence is a major factor in their growing demand. Cavapoos possess a natural inclination toward human interaction, often sensing emotional states and responding with gentle companionship. This sensitivity makes them particularly attractive as therapy animals, emotional support companions, and family pets who can adapt to various social dynamics. Their gentle disposition, coupled with an eagerness to please, allows them to form strong bonds with individuals across age groups, making them especially valuable in households with children or elderly family members.

Additionally, the Cavapoo represents the evolution of designer hybrid breeds in modern pet ownership. While crossbreeds have existed for centuries, intentional breeding for companion traits has gained prominence in recent years. The Cavapoo is a prime example of this trend, carefully bred to combine the best characteristics of two highly compatible breeds. This intentional design means that owners can often expect more predictable traits in behavior, temperament, and size, making it easier to integrate the dog into family life.

Purpose of This Book

The purpose of this guide is to provide a thorough, accessible, and practical resource for anyone considering a Cavapoo as a pet. Many people are drawn to Cavapoos because of their appealing appearance and affectionate nature, but owning a dog is a significant commitment that extends beyond initial charm. This book seeks to prepare owners to understand the breed fully, anticipate their needs, and provide responsible, long-term care. From selecting a puppy or adopting an adult dog to providing daily nutrition, grooming, mental stimulation, and veterinary care, this guide is designed to cover every aspect of Cavapoo ownership.

By reading this book, prospective owners will gain insight into the breed's temperament, behavioral tendencies, and unique needs. Knowledge is essential to ensuring the well-being of a Cavapoo, as these dogs thrive on consistency, social interaction, and emotional support. Understanding the breed's characteristics helps avoid common challenges, such as separation anxiety, overexcitement, or health-related issues, while promoting positive, enriching interactions between dog and owner.

Furthermore, this book emphasizes ethical and responsible ownership. With the popularity of designer breeds like the Cavapoo, there has been a rise in unregulated breeding practices, sometimes prioritizing profit over the welfare of dogs. Readers will learn how to select reputable breeders, consider adoption opportunities, and make informed decisions that benefit both the dog and the broader community. By establishing a foundation of ethical practices, owners can contribute to the long-term health and sustainability of the breed, ensuring that Cavapoos continue to be celebrated for their positive traits rather than exploited for trends or financial gain.

Appeal to Families

Families are among the primary groups drawn to Cavapoos. The breed's gentle, affectionate nature makes it an ideal companion for children. Cavapoos typically exhibit patience, sociability, and adaptability, traits that allow them to coexist harmoniously with younger family members. They enjoy interactive play, respond well to training, and often form strong, lasting bonds with children, providing both emotional support and companionship.

Children, in particular, benefit from the presence of a Cavapoo. Learning to care for a dog teaches responsibility, empathy, and nurturing skills. In many households, children are involved in feeding, grooming, and training activities, which fosters a sense of accomplishment and strengthens the family bond. Cavapoos are resilient and forgiving, but it is important for parents to supervise interactions to ensure the dog is treated gently and respectfully. In families with multiple children, the dog can also act as a calming presence, teaching patience and offering a reliable source of emotional support.

Beyond play and companionship, Cavapoos often provide a sense of security and stability for families. Their keen senses and alertness allow them to be aware of household activities without being excessively territorial or aggressive. This balance makes them ideal for households where socialization and interaction are frequent, yet a calm, steady temperament is appreciated.

Appeal to Seniors

Seniors also find Cavapoos particularly appealing. Their manageable size, moderate exercise needs, and affectionate temperament align well with the lifestyles of older adults. For seniors, a Cavapoo can offer companionship, reduce feelings of isolation, and provide gentle encouragement for physical activity. Daily walks, interactive play, and grooming routines can help maintain both the owner's and the dog's physical health while promoting mental stimulation and social engagement.

Cavapoos provide emotional stability and companionship in a way that can improve overall quality of life for seniors. Their intuitive nature allows them to sense emotional states and offer comfort, which can alleviate feelings of loneliness or anxiety. Furthermore, the breed's moderate energy levels are ideal for owners who may not be able to manage highly active dogs but still want a companion that engages in play, exercise, and interaction.

Appeal as Therapy and Emotional Support Animals

Beyond traditional household settings, Cavapoos have gained recognition as therapy and emotional support animals. Their empathetic nature, intelligence, and gentle disposition make them suitable for assisting individuals dealing with anxiety, depression, or other emotional challenges. Cavapoos are capable of forming strong, trusting relationships, responding to subtle cues in human behavior, and offering comfort through companionship.

These traits are particularly valuable in clinical and therapeutic environments, such as hospitals, nursing homes, and schools. Organizations that incorporate therapy dogs often look for breeds that are calm, adaptable, and sociable—qualities that Cavapoos frequently exhibit. While formal certification is required for professional therapy work, many Cavapoos naturally demonstrate the temperament suited for emotional support, even without certification, making them invaluable members of households seeking emotional connection and comfort.

The breed's ability to sense human emotions and provide reassurance is one of its defining qualities. Owners often report that Cavapoos are especially attentive during moments of distress, providing warmth and companionship through physical closeness or gentle interaction. This emotional intelligence elevates the breed beyond a traditional pet, highlighting its potential to enrich human lives in meaningful ways.

Setting the Tone for Responsible Ownership

Owning a Cavapoo is a privilege that comes with responsibilities. While their affectionate nature and charming demeanor can make ownership appear effortless, responsible care involves planning, commitment, and consistent attention. This guide underscores the importance of understanding the breed's physical, mental, and emotional needs before bringing a Cavapoo into your home.

Responsible ownership begins with education. Understanding the breed's exercise requirements, grooming needs, nutritional considerations, and common health concerns is essential for preventing issues and ensuring a long, fulfilling life for your dog. This guide will provide practical steps for integrating a Cavapoo into your lifestyle, maintaining their well-being, and nurturing a strong, trusting bond.

Moreover, responsible ownership involves ethical decision-making. Prospective owners must consider the source of their Cavapoo, evaluate breeders carefully, and explore adoption opportunities. Prioritizing the dog's welfare over convenience or trends fosters a culture of care and helps maintain the integrity of the breed for future generations.

Long-Term Care and Commitment

A Cavapoo's lifespan typically ranges from 10 to 15 years, sometimes longer with attentive care. This long-term commitment requires planning for health care, nutrition, exercise, grooming, and emotional well-being throughout the dog's life stages—from puppyhood to senior years. Prospective owners must be prepared to invest time, effort, and resources consistently to provide a stable, enriching environment.

This book also highlights the importance of adaptability and ongoing learning. As dogs grow and their needs evolve, owners must adjust routines, provide age-appropriate care, and maintain vigilance for health changes. Lifelong learning about the breed, behavior, and advancements in veterinary care ensures that Cavapoos receive optimal support, enhancing their quality of life and deepening the bond with their human companions.

Overview of the Book's Structure

This book is organized to guide readers step by step through the journey of Cavapoo ownership. It begins with understanding the breed's history, physical traits, and temperament, then explores suitability for various lifestyles. Subsequent chapters provide practical guidance on selecting a dog, preparing your home, feeding, exercise, grooming, training, and veterinary care. Later chapters focus on enrichment, emotional health, traveling, and long-term responsibilities, culminating in a comprehensive view of what it means to be a responsible Cavapoo owner.

Each chapter is designed to be both educational and practical, equipping readers with actionable advice and insights grounded in real-world experience. By the end of the book, readers will be prepared not only to provide a loving home but also to nurture a thriving relationship with their Cavapoo, ensuring the dog's well-being, happiness, and longevity.

Conclusion

The Cavapoo is more than a pet—it is a companion, a source of comfort, and a member of the family. Their combination of affectionate temperament, intelligence, adaptability, and emotional sensitivity makes them highly appealing to families, seniors, and therapy seekers alike. However, the joy of owning a Cavapoo comes with the responsibility of understanding, planning, and committing to long-term care.

This book begins the journey by equipping you with the knowledge needed to make informed, ethical decisions, ensuring that your Cavapoo thrives in a safe, loving, and enriched environment. As you continue through the chapters, you will gain insight into the breed's unique traits, practical care requirements, and strategies for building a lasting, fulfilling relationship. By embracing the principles of responsible ownership outlined here, you can experience the true rewards of life with a Cavapoo—a bond built on love, trust, and mutual enrichment that lasts for years to come.

Chapter 2

History and Origins

Understanding the origins of a breed is essential for appreciating its behavior, temperament, and care requirements. The Cavapoo, also referred to as Cavoodle, is a hybrid breed created by crossing the Cavalier King Charles Spaniel with the Poodle. While hybrid or designer breeds are sometimes viewed as modern inventions, the Cavapoo's creation was deliberate, guided by specific goals aimed at producing a companion dog that blends intelligence, gentleness, and adaptability. By examining its history, parentage, and the objectives of its breeders, prospective owners can gain a clear understanding of what makes this breed so uniquely suited to modern families.

The Legacy of the Cavalier King Charles Spaniel

The Cavalier King Charles Spaniel is a breed with deep historical roots. Dating back to the 16th and 17th centuries, these dogs were favored companions of European nobility, particularly in England. They were often seen perched on the laps of kings and queens, providing both comfort and companionship. Their appeal extended beyond their small stature; Cavaliers are known for their expressive eyes, gentle nature, and unwavering loyalty.

Historically, these dogs were bred for their temperament rather than athletic ability. They excelled in forming strong emotional bonds with humans, displaying patience and sociability. Children and adults alike were drawn to their affectionate personalities, which made them ideal family companions. The Cavalier's temperament emphasizes calmness, empathy, and sensitivity—traits that have become fundamental to the Cavapoo's personality.

The Distinct Qualities of the Poodle

The Poodle, in contrast, has a history rooted in working roles. Originally developed in Germany as a water retriever, the Poodle later became highly popular in France, where it gained recognition for its intelligence, elegance, and versatility. Poodles are renowned for their problem-solving abilities, trainability, and highly adaptable nature. They possess a distinctive curly coat that sheds minimally, making them suitable for households concerned about allergens.

Poodles were bred to perform tasks requiring mental agility, such as retrieving waterfowl or assisting in various forms of hunting. Their intelligence and responsiveness made them easy to train, and over time, they became favored as companion animals. The breed's hypoallergenic coat, combined with a high capacity for learning, makes it a natural candidate for hybridization aimed at producing a family-friendly dog with minimal shedding.

The Birth of the Cavapoo

The Cavapoo emerged as a deliberate hybrid in the late 20th century, primarily in Australia, before gaining popularity in other regions including the United States, Europe, and Asia. The intent behind creating the Cavapoo was clear: to merge the Cavalier's warmth and gentleness with the Poodle's intelligence and low-shedding coat. Breeders envisioned a dog that could serve as a loyal family companion, adapt to a variety of living situations, and provide emotional support across different households.

The early generations of Cavapoos typically involved crossing a purebred Cavalier King Charles Spaniel with a purebred Poodle, producing an F1 hybrid. Subsequent breeding strategies, such as backcrossing with one of the parent breeds or mating F1 Cavapoos together, were employed to stabilize traits such as temperament, size, and coat type. Because hybrid genetics are inherently variable, each Cavapoo may inherit different characteristics from its parents, resulting in unique appearances and personalities. This unpredictability is part of the breed's charm and emphasizes the importance of selecting dogs from reputable breeders who prioritize health and temperament.

Goals of the Cavapoo Crossbreed

The development of the Cavapoo was guided by specific goals aimed at creating the ideal companion dog. These objectives include:

1. Temperament: Breeders sought to produce a dog that is affectionate, gentle, and socially adaptable. The Cavalier's sensitivity complements the Poodle's intelligence, resulting in a breed that is calm yet responsive to its environment. Cavapoos tend to be people-oriented, forming strong bonds with family members and often seeking companionship throughout the day.

2. Intelligence: The Poodle's high intelligence ensures that Cavapoos are highly trainable. They learn commands quickly, excel in obedience training, and engage enthusiastically in problem-solving activities. This makes them suitable not only as household pets but also as therapy or emotional support animals.

3. Low-Shedding Coat: Many modern households seek dogs with minimal shedding, either due to allergies or cleanliness concerns. The Poodle's low-shedding gene, when combined with the Cavalier's coat, produces a dog with either wavy or curly fur that sheds minimally. While no dog is entirely hypoallergenic, Cavapoos are widely regarded as an ideal choice for allergy-sensitive families.

4. Adaptability: Cavapoos were bred to thrive in a range of environments, from small apartments to larger homes with yards. Their balanced energy levels and adaptable temperament make them suitable for various household dynamics, whether living alone with a single owner or as part of an active family with children.

5. Companionship: Above all, Cavapoos were designed to be companions. They are emotionally attuned to their owners, capable of sensing moods, providing comfort, and participating actively in family life. This combination of traits makes them highly desirable as lifelong family pets.

Variations Based on Poodle Type

The size and energy levels of Cavapoos can vary depending on whether the Poodle parent is a Toy or Miniature. These variations affect not only the dog's size but also aspects of behavior and adaptability.

Toy Cavapoos are generally smaller, weighing between 6 and 12 pounds and standing around 9 to 12 inches tall. These dogs are ideal for apartment living or for owners seeking a compact companion. Toy Cavapoos retain the breed's affectionate and intelligent traits but may be slightly more delicate, requiring careful handling with young children.

Miniature Cavapoos are slightly larger, typically weighing 12 to 20 pounds and standing 12 to 15 inches tall. These dogs often have a bit more energy and resilience, making them suitable for households with active families or children. The slightly larger size can make training and daily exercise easier to manage compared to Toy Cavapoos.

Understanding the Poodle type used in breeding allows prospective owners to match the dog to their lifestyle and living arrangements. It also provides insight into potential energy levels, exercise requirements, and handling considerations.

Global Popularity and Cultural Impact

Since their creation, Cavapoos have gained international recognition as ideal companion dogs. Their combination of intelligence, gentle temperament, and low-shedding coat has made them popular in Australia, the United States, Europe, and Asia. The breed is frequently featured in media, social networks, and pet-focused publications, which has further boosted its visibility.

Cavapoos are also increasingly utilized in therapy and emotional support roles. Their attentiveness to human emotions, combined with a small and manageable size, allows them to provide comfort in hospitals, nursing homes, and schools. Many organizations seeking therapy dogs favor Cavapoos because they respond calmly to new environments, interact safely with people of all ages, and offer consistent emotional support.

Genetic Considerations and Health Awareness

Because Cavapoos are hybrid dogs, their traits can vary widely. Physical characteristics, coat type, size, and temperament depend on which parent's genes are dominant. This variation highlights the importance of selecting dogs from responsible breeders who conduct health screenings and prioritize temperament.

Reputable breeders often test for common health concerns in both parent breeds, such as heart disease, hip dysplasia, eye conditions, and patellar luxation. Understanding the genetic background and potential health issues of both parents can help owners anticipate challenges and provide proactive care, ensuring that their Cavapoo enjoys a long, healthy life.

The Cavapoo as a Modern Companion

The Cavapoo represents a thoughtful approach to dog breeding, blending the best qualities of two beloved breeds to meet the needs of contemporary households. They are intelligent, affectionate, adaptable, and emotionally perceptive, making them exceptional family pets, therapy animals, and companions for seniors. Their combination of traits ensures they integrate well into a variety of home environments, from urban apartments to rural estates.

Prospective owners benefit greatly from understanding the breed's origins. Recognizing the purpose behind their creation allows owners to appreciate their behavior, anticipate needs, and provide an enriched environment that supports both physical and emotional well-being.

Conclusion

The Cavapoo's history and origins reveal a breed carefully developed to meet the needs of modern pet owners. By combining the Cavalier King Charles Spaniel's affectionate temperament with the Poodle's intelligence and low-shedding coat, breeders created a companion dog that thrives in family homes, apartments, and therapeutic settings. Variations based on Poodle type, along with careful attention to genetics, ensure that each Cavapoo possesses a unique combination of traits while remaining consistent in emotional warmth and adaptability.

Understanding the Cavapoo's heritage is fundamental for prospective owners. It provides insight into their behavior, health, and care requirements while emphasizing the importance of responsible ownership. As this guide progresses, the knowledge of the breed's origins will serve as a foundation for selecting, raising, and nurturing a Cavapoo that will provide years of companionship, joy, and emotional connection.

Chapter 3

Physical Characteristics and Appearance

One of the most appealing aspects of the Cavapoo is its physical charm. From expressive eyes to soft, luxurious coats, the breed's appearance reflects its hybrid heritage, blending the Cavalier King Charles Spaniel's elegance with the Poodle's distinctive features. Understanding a Cavapoo's physical characteristics is essential for prospective owners, as these traits impact care requirements, grooming routines, and expectations for size and temperament. This chapter explores size ranges, coat types, colors, and the influence of hybrid genetics, providing guidance on predicting puppy appearance and preparing for long-term care.

Size Ranges: Toy vs. Miniature Cavapoos

The size of a Cavapoo depends largely on the Poodle parent used in breeding. Poodles come in Toy, Miniature, and Standard sizes, though Cavapoos are typically bred using Toy or Miniature Poodles to maintain a manageable companion dog.

Toy **Cavapoo:**
Toy Cavapoos are the smaller variation, typically weighing between 6 and 12 pounds and standing around 9 to 12 inches tall at the shoulder. Their small stature makes them ideal for apartment living, smaller households, or seniors seeking a compact companion. Despite their diminutive size, Toy Cavapoos retain the breed's characteristic energy, intelligence, and affectionate temperament. Prospective owners should be mindful that smaller dogs can be more delicate, requiring careful handling, especially around young children or other pets.

Miniature **Cavapoo:**
Miniature Cavapoos are slightly larger, weighing between 12 and 20 pounds and standing 12 to 15 inches tall. Their increased size often brings greater resilience and slightly higher energy

levels, making them well-suited for families with children or households where the dog will participate in more active play. Miniature Cavapoos generally maintain the same affectionate and intelligent qualities as Toy Cavapoos but may be easier to train for certain activities due to their slightly sturdier build.

Predicting   Adult   Size:
 Estimating the adult size of a Cavapoo puppy can be challenging due to hybrid genetics. Breeders often consider the sizes of both parents, growth patterns, and lineage to make an educated guess. As a general rule, a Toy Cavapoo puppy may reach about 90–95% of its adult size by six to eight months of age, while Miniature Cavapoos may continue to fill out until 12 months. Observing growth patterns during the first few months, along with proper nutrition and health monitoring, helps owners anticipate the dog's eventual size and adjust feeding, exercise, and space accordingly.

Coat Types: Wavy, Curly, and Silky

One of the most distinctive features of the Cavapoo is its coat, which reflects the influence of both parent breeds. Unlike purebred dogs with predictable coat types, Cavapoos can display a variety of textures and patterns due to their hybrid genetics.

Wavy   Coats:

Wavy coats are perhaps the most common among Cavapoos. This texture combines elements of the Cavalier's silky hair and the Poodle's curl, resulting in loose, flowing waves. Wavy coats are soft to the touch, visually appealing, and moderately easy to maintain with regular brushing to prevent tangles. Owners often find wavy coats strikingly elegant, offering a balance between appearance and manageability.

Curly   Coats:

Curly coats are more reminiscent of the Poodle parent, featuring tight curls that may vary from loose ringlets to compact spirals. Curly coats are highly valued for their low-shedding qualities, making them an excellent choice for allergy-sensitive households. However, these coats require consistent grooming, including brushing multiple times per week and regular trimming to prevent matting. Curly-coated Cavapoos often retain the Poodle's hypoallergenic properties more strongly than their wavy or silky-coated siblings.

Silky   Coats:

Some Cavapoos inherit a straighter, silkier coat, reflecting stronger Cavalier influence. Silky coats are soft, shiny, and prone to tangling if not properly maintained. They shed minimally compared to pure Cavaliers, but grooming routines should include gentle brushing and occasional trimming to maintain smoothness and prevent knots, especially behind the ears and around the legs.

Grooming   Considerations:

Regardless of coat type, regular grooming is essential for Cavapoos. Daily or every-other-day brushing helps reduce matting and tangling, distributes natural oils, and keeps the coat looking healthy. Curly or wavy coats may require professional grooming every six to eight weeks, including trimming and styling to maintain shape and comfort. Owners should also monitor ears, teeth, and nails, as these areas are prone to health issues if neglected.

Coat Colors and Patterns

Cavapoos display a wide variety of colors and patterns due to hybridization. Some common colors include:

- **Blonde or Cream:** Soft, light-colored coats that can range from pale ivory to rich honey shades. These colors often resemble the Poodle parent and are visually striking.
- **Red or Apricot:** Warm, reddish tones that may appear solid or mixed with subtle shading. This coloration often carries the warmth of the Cavalier's chestnut hues.
- **Black or Chocolate:** Deep, rich colors that may include tan points, reflecting Poodle influence. These darker colors often contrast beautifully with the eyes and nose, giving a distinctive appearance.
- **Tri-color or Parti:** Multi-colored coats featuring combinations of white, black, tan, or red. These patterns are common in first-generation hybrids and can result in striking, unique appearances.
- **Blenheim and Other Cavalier Patterns:** Some Cavapoos inherit traditional Cavalier markings,

including the Blenheim pattern (chestnut and white), which adds to the breed's charm and visual appeal.

It is important to note that puppy coats can change as the dog matures. Many Cavapoos are born with lighter or muted colors that deepen or develop additional markings over the first year. Predicting the adult coat color requires careful observation of the puppy's parents and understanding the genetics involved in coat inheritance.

Hybrid Genetics and Appearance

Hybrid genetics play a crucial role in determining a Cavapoo's physical traits. Unlike purebred dogs with predictable features, Cavapoos inherit a combination of genes from both parent breeds, creating variety in size, coat type, color, and facial structure. This genetic diversity ensures that each Cavapoo is unique, even within the same litter.

Facial   **Features:**
Cavapoos often inherit the Cavalier's expressive eyes and rounded face, combined with the Poodle's refined snout and alert expression. The result is a soft, engaging facial appearance

that conveys both intelligence and affection. The muzzle may be slightly longer than a Cavalier's, providing a balance between expression and functionality.

Body   Structure:
Cavapoos typically exhibit a sturdy yet compact body. They inherit the Cavalier's graceful proportions while benefiting from the Poodle's strength and poise. This combination produces a dog that is agile, comfortable in domestic settings, and capable of moderate activity levels without excessive strain.

Tail   and   Ears:
The tail is often medium-length, with a gentle plume that reflects both parent breeds. Ears can range from long and floppy to slightly shorter and wavier, depending on the dominant genetic traits. Regular grooming of the ears is necessary to prevent infections, especially for dogs with longer, wavy, or curly hair.

Tips for Predicting Puppy Traits

While hybrid genetics create variety, there are strategies to anticipate a puppy's physical traits:

1. **Examine the Parents:** Observing the coat type, size, color, and temperament of both parents provides valuable clues about the puppy's potential appearance.

2. **Consider Poodle Type:** Knowing whether the Poodle parent is Toy or Miniature can help estimate adult size and energy levels.

3. **Understand Coat Inheritance:** Curly coats are often dominant over straight coats, meaning puppies with at least one Poodle parent carrying the curly gene are likely to inherit curls or waves.

4. **Observe Puppy Development:** Puppies' coat texture, color, and body proportions often begin to solidify around three to six months of age, providing more accurate predictions for adulthood.

5. **Expect Variability:** Even within a single litter, puppies may differ in size, coat type, and markings. Hybrid diversity is part of the breed's charm, and no two Cavapoos are identical.

Physical Traits and Lifestyle Considerations

Understanding a Cavapoo's physical characteristics is not only a matter of aesthetics but also essential for daily care. Size and coat type influence exercise needs, grooming routines, and dietary considerations. Small Toy Cavapoos may require less physical space but more attentive handling, while Miniature Cavapoos may thrive with increased activity and outdoor play. Similarly, curly-coated dogs require regular brushing and professional grooming, while wavy or silky coats may be more manageable but still benefit from routine care.

Proper attention to physical traits ensures the dog's comfort, health, and overall well-being. Owners who understand these factors can provide a supportive environment that caters to their Cavapoo's unique needs, fostering a longer, happier life.

Conclusion

The Cavapoo's physical characteristics are a captivating blend of its Cavalier King Charles Spaniel and Poodle heritage. From size and coat type to color and facial features, each dog is unique, reflecting the rich diversity of hybrid genetics. By understanding these traits, prospective owners can make informed decisions about which puppy suits their household, anticipate grooming and exercise needs, and provide appropriate care throughout the dog's life. The charm of the Cavapoo lies not only in its appearance but also in the thoughtful combination of traits that make it a versatile, affectionate, and intelligent companion. In the next chapters, we will explore temperament, behavior, and the practical aspects of raising a Cavapoo, building on the foundation of knowledge about its physical form.

Chapter 4

Temperament and Personality

A dog's temperament is arguably one of the most important factors influencing its suitability for a household. The Cavapoo's charm extends far beyond its physical appearance; it lies in the combination of emotional intelligence, affectionate behavior, and adaptive personality traits inherited from its parent breeds. Understanding what to expect from a Cavapoo in daily life is essential for prospective owners, as it allows for preparation, realistic expectations, and the cultivation of a strong, lasting bond between dog and human family members.

A Blend of Parent Traits

The Cavapoo inherits behavioral characteristics from both the Cavalier King Charles Spaniel and the Poodle, resulting in a hybrid dog that combines the best traits of both. While every dog is unique, breeders and owners often note recurring themes in Cavapoo behavior:

From the Cavalier King Charles Spaniel:

- **Affectionate Nature:** Cavaliers are renowned for their gentle and loving temperament. This translates to Cavapoos being highly people-oriented, often seeking closeness with family members and forming deep emotional bonds.
- **Social Orientation:** Cavaliers enjoy interacting with humans and other animals, making them ideal for households with children, multiple pets, or frequent visitors.
- **Calm and Patient:** The Cavalier's temperament is generally relaxed and patient, lending itself well to family life and low-stress environments.

From the Poodle:

- **Intelligence and Problem-Solving:** Poodles are one of the most intelligent dog breeds, and Cavapoos often inherit their ability to learn quickly, respond to training, and adapt to new situations.

- **Alertness and Curiosity:** Poodles are naturally inquisitive and aware of their surroundings. Cavapoos may exhibit similar curiosity, exploring their environment with interest and alertness.

- **Energy Balance:** While Poodles can be highly energetic, their intelligence allows them to channel energy appropriately. Cavapoos often exhibit a balanced energy level, capable of playful bursts but also enjoying quiet time with their owners.

Attachment and Bonding

Cavapoos are often described as "velcro dogs" due to their strong attachment to their human family. They thrive on companionship and may become anxious if left alone for long periods. This deep attachment makes them excellent emotional support dogs, as they are sensitive to the moods and needs of their owners.

Owners often report that Cavapoos follow them from room to room, seek attention during leisure activities, and respond positively to affectionate interactions. This bond can be highly rewarding but also requires responsible management. For instance, separation anxiety can develop if the dog is consistently left alone, underscoring the importance of gradual training and mental stimulation to promote independence.

Playfulness and Social Interaction

Cavapoos are playful without being overly rambunctious. They enjoy interactive play, such as fetch, tug-of-war, and gentle games with children or other pets. Their playfulness is often tempered by intelligence, allowing them to follow rules and learn commands even in playful situations.

Socialization is critical for Cavapoos, particularly during puppyhood. Exposing them to various people, environments, and other animals fosters confidence, reduces the likelihood of fear-based behavior, and strengthens their social skills. Well-socialized Cavapoos are friendly, adaptable, and able to navigate a wide range of social settings, from family gatherings to visits to the park or dog-friendly public spaces.

Intelligence and Trainability

One of the standout traits of the Cavapoo is intelligence. Inherited primarily from the Poodle parent, this intelligence makes them quick learners and highly trainable. Cavapoos excel in obedience training, can learn tricks, and often respond well to advanced training, including agility and therapy dog work.

Their intelligence also manifests in problem-solving and curiosity. Cavapoos may attempt to open doors, retrieve hidden objects, or explore new areas, requiring consistent guidance and engagement from their owners. Mental stimulation is essential for Cavapoos to prevent boredom, which can lead to destructive behaviors such as chewing or digging. Puzzle toys, interactive play, and obedience exercises are excellent ways to keep their minds active.

Adaptability

Cavapoos are remarkably adaptable, capable of thriving in various living situations. Their size allows them to fit comfortably into apartments or smaller homes, while their temperament ensures they are content in quieter environments or active households. They adjust well to changes in routine, new family members, and even travel, provided they are introduced gradually and with care.

Despite this adaptability, Cavapoos benefit from consistent structure. Routine feeding, exercise, and training help maintain stability, prevent anxiety, and support emotional well-being. Owners who provide predictability alongside flexibility often find that their Cavapoo remains calm, confident, and happy in diverse situations.

Emotional Sensitivity and Awareness

Cavapoos are highly intuitive, often sensing the emotional state of their owners. They respond to cues such as tone of voice, body language, and facial expressions, making them excellent companions for individuals seeking emotional support. This sensitivity also means that Cavapoos can be affected by household tension, loud noises, or stressful events.

Owners often find that Cavapoos will offer comfort when someone is upset, cuddle for reassurance, or exhibit playful behavior to uplift a family member's mood. This emotional responsiveness strengthens the bond between dog and owner but also highlights the importance of providing a calm, supportive environment.

Daily Life Expectations

In daily life, owners can expect the Cavapoo to:

- **Seek companionship:** They enjoy spending time with family members and may follow their owners around the house.
- **Engage in moderate play:** Cavapoos enjoy interactive games, walks, and short bursts of energetic play, balanced by periods of relaxation.

- **Respond to training:** They learn commands quickly, enjoy mental stimulation, and often excel in obedience or agility training.
- **Socialize well:** With proper socialization, Cavapoos are friendly with children, adults, and other pets.
- **Provide emotional support:** Their sensitivity to human emotions makes them excellent companions for individuals seeking comfort or therapy dogs.

While generally easygoing, Cavapoos require attentive care, including mental and physical stimulation, social interaction, and consistent guidance. Without these, even a well-tempered dog can develop behavioral issues such as excessive barking, separation anxiety, or minor destructive behaviors.

Common Behavioral Traits in the Home

- **Affectionate Nature:** Cavapoos often seek physical closeness, enjoying cuddles and lap time.
- **Playful Curiosity:** They may explore rooms, investigate new objects, and engage actively with toys.

- **Gentle Interaction:** Particularly with children and seniors, Cavapoos are patient, non-aggressive, and careful in their play.
- **Vocalization:** While not typically excessive barkers, Cavapoos may alert owners to visitors or unfamiliar noises.
- **Loyalty:** They demonstrate strong bonds with their family, often showing loyalty and attachment to one primary caregiver or several close family members.

Influence of Hybrid Genetics

Hybrid genetics play a central role in shaping the Cavapoo's personality. Because the breed combines traits from both parent breeds, temperament can vary between individuals. Some Cavapoos may lean more toward the Cavalier side, exhibiting calm, gentle behavior and strong emotional attachment, while others may inherit a higher degree of Poodle energy, curiosity, and playfulness. Understanding this variability allows owners to anticipate the dog's needs, tailor training methods, and provide appropriate socialization.

Responsible breeders often select parent dogs with stable temperaments to minimize undesirable traits and produce puppies with consistent behavioral patterns. Observing both parents' behavior can provide insights into the puppy's potential personality, helping owners make informed decisions when choosing a companion.

Preparing for a Cavapoo's Personality

Prospective owners can take several steps to nurture a well-rounded Cavapoo:

- **Early Socialization:** Introduce the puppy to various people, pets, and environments to promote confidence and reduce fearfulness.
- **Positive Reinforcement Training:** Cavapoos respond well to rewards-based training, which reinforces desirable behaviors without causing stress or fear.
- **Mental Stimulation:** Engage their intelligence with puzzle toys, learning games, and interactive play to prevent boredom and destructive habits.

- **Consistent Routine:** Provide structure in feeding, exercise, and training, which supports emotional stability and reduces anxiety.
- **Affection and Attention:** Cavapoos thrive on human connection, so providing daily affection and engagement is essential for happiness.

Conclusion

The Cavapoo's temperament and personality make it a truly remarkable companion. By blending the Cavalier King Charles Spaniel's affectionate, gentle nature with the Poodle's intelligence, adaptability, and curiosity, the breed offers a unique combination of traits that appeal to families, seniors, and therapy seekers alike. Understanding these characteristics helps prospective owners prepare for daily life with a Cavapoo, anticipate behavioral tendencies, and foster a bond built on trust, love, and mutual enrichment.

Cavapoos are playful yet gentle, intelligent yet sensitive, and adaptable yet loyal. They excel in social settings, respond well to training, and provide unmatched companionship. By appreciating the nuances of their temperament, owners can create a nurturing environment that allows the Cavapoo to flourish, ensuring a long, fulfilling life for both dog and family.

Chapter 5

Is a Cavapoo Right for You?

Bringing a Cavapoo into your life is a commitment that requires careful consideration. While the breed's charm, intelligence, and affectionate nature make it an appealing choice for many households, not every lifestyle is suited to their needs. Understanding the breed's requirements—including time, attention, activity levels, and emotional needs—is essential to determine whether a Cavapoo will thrive in your home. This chapter evaluates lifestyle compatibility, highlights considerations for different types of owners, and provides guidance for first-time dog owners.

Lifestyle Compatibility: Who Thrives with a Cavapoo?

The Cavapoo is versatile, adapting to a variety of living situations and household dynamics. Its size, temperament, and activity levels allow it to fit well in both urban and suburban settings. However, certain lifestyles are better suited than others.

Families   with   Children:
Cavapoos are excellent family pets. Their gentle nature, patience, and social orientation make them ideal companions for children. Cavaliers contribute calmness and affectionate interaction, while Poodles add intelligence and playfulness, allowing Cavapoos to engage with kids safely and energetically. Families should supervise interactions between young children and small Toy Cavapoos to prevent accidental injury to the dog. Miniature Cavapoos are typically sturdier, making them more resilient for active play. A household with children benefits from early socialization, consistent training, and structured playtime to ensure positive interactions.

Seniors   and   Retirees:
Cavapoos are well-suited to seniors, offering companionship, emotional support, and manageable exercise needs. Their moderate energy levels allow for short walks and interactive play without being overly demanding. Their affectionate nature provides emotional comfort, reducing feelings of loneliness and

fostering well-being. Seniors should consider their ability to provide daily care, including grooming, feeding, and veterinary visits, particularly for curly-coated Cavapoos that require regular maintenance.

Apartment   Dwellers:

Due to their compact size, Toy and Miniature Cavapoos can thrive in apartments or smaller homes. While they do not require extensive space, they need mental stimulation and opportunities for short outdoor walks. Noise management is another consideration; Cavapoos are alert dogs and may bark at unfamiliar sounds. Apartment living works best when owners provide consistent exercise, interactive play, and socialization to channel the dog's energy appropriately.

Allergy-Sensitive   Households:

Cavapoos are often chosen by households concerned about allergies due to their low-shedding coats. While no dog is entirely hypoallergenic, the breed's Poodle ancestry often results in a wavy or curly coat that produces less dander and hair in the home. Families with mild allergies may find Cavapoos more suitable than breeds that shed heavily. It is recommended to spend time with the breed before committing to ensure individual reactions are manageable.

Active   Households: Miniature Cavapoos in particular enjoy moderate activity and benefit from daily walks, playtime, and mental stimulation. While they are not high-energy working dogs, they enjoy participating in family activities such as hiking, games in the yard, or interactive training. Families who are active and enjoy involving their dog in daily routines will find the Cavapoo highly engaging and responsive.

Time Commitment

Cavapoos are companion dogs, meaning they thrive on attention, affection, and interaction. Prospective owners must be prepared for the time commitment involved:

- **Daily Interaction:** Cavapoos seek companionship throughout the day and may become anxious or bored if left alone for extended periods. Even a few hours without human contact can lead to separation anxiety in some dogs.

- **Exercise Needs:** Short walks, play sessions, and mental stimulation are necessary daily. While their physical exercise needs are moderate compared to high-energy breeds, they still require consistent activity to remain healthy and balanced.

- **Grooming:** The time spent on grooming depends on coat type. Curly-coated Cavapoos need regular brushing and professional trimming every six to eight weeks, while wavy or silky coats require slightly less maintenance. Neglecting grooming can lead to matting, discomfort, and skin problems.

- **Training:** Daily training sessions using positive reinforcement help maintain obedience, mental engagement, and good behavior. Their intelligence makes them quick learners, but consistent guidance is necessary to prevent boredom-related behaviors such as chewing or digging.

Emotional Needs

Cavapoos are emotionally sensitive dogs that respond to their owners' moods and require a supportive environment. Their needs include:

- **Companionship:** These dogs thrive on social interaction and do best when integrated into family life.
- **Mental Engagement:** Puzzles, obedience training, and interactive toys provide the stimulation they need.
- **Consistency:** A structured routine reduces stress and supports emotional well-being.
- **Affection:** Cavapoos are highly affectionate and enjoy cuddling, lap time, and positive attention.

Owners must be ready to invest time and energy into meeting these emotional needs. Dogs that are neglected, left alone for long periods, or deprived of interaction may develop anxiety, excessive barking, or other behavioral issues.

Suitability for First-Time Dog Owners

Cavapoos are generally considered suitable for first-time dog owners due to their trainable nature, moderate exercise needs, and social temperament. Key considerations include:

- **Training Patience:** While intelligent, Cavapoos still require consistent training and reinforcement. First-time owners must be prepared for the commitment to teach basic commands, potty training, and socialization.

- **Grooming Knowledge:** Understanding coat care is essential. Even low-maintenance coats require routine brushing and occasional professional grooming.

- **Awareness of Emotional Needs:** Owners must recognize the breed's attachment tendencies and plan for companionship and mental stimulation.

- **Veterinary Care:** First-time owners should familiarize themselves with preventive health measures, vaccinations, dental care, and monitoring for common Cavapoo health issues such as heart murmurs or patellar luxation.

With proper preparation, first-time owners can enjoy a rewarding experience with a Cavapoo, benefiting from the breed's intelligence, affection, and adaptability.

Challenges to Consider

While Cavapoos are well-suited for many households, there are challenges to consider:

- **Separation Anxiety:** Their strong attachment to family members can lead to anxiety if left alone frequently. Gradual training and enrichment activities can mitigate this risk.
- **Grooming Demands:** Curly or wavy coats require regular care to prevent tangling and matting. Neglect can lead to discomfort and skin issues.
- **Moderate Energy Levels:** Cavapoos are playful and curious, requiring regular interaction. Boredom may result in minor destructive behavior.
- **Health Awareness:** While generally healthy, hybrid vigor does not eliminate the risk of inherited conditions.

Responsible breeding and regular veterinary care are essential.

Making an Informed Decision

Determining whether a Cavapoo is the right dog for you involves evaluating your lifestyle, resources, and commitment level. Consider the following questions:

1. Can you provide daily attention, exercise, and mental stimulation?
2. Is your household environment suitable for a small, social dog?
3. Are you prepared for regular grooming and coat maintenance?
4. Do you understand the emotional needs of a companion breed?
5. Can you accommodate the potential for separation anxiety and plan for gradual acclimation?

Answering these questions honestly will help prospective owners determine if a Cavapoo will thrive in their home. The breed rewards attentive, engaged owners with affection, loyalty, and companionship, but it requires commitment, patience, and care.

Summary

Cavapoos are versatile, affectionate, and intelligent dogs suited to a variety of households. They excel with families, seniors, apartment dwellers, and first-time dog owners who can meet their emotional, mental, and physical needs. Their low-shedding coats, moderate energy levels, and adaptability make them appealing to allergy-sensitive households or owners seeking a companion dog that is both engaging and manageable.

However, Cavapoos require daily interaction, socialization, grooming, and mental stimulation. Owners must be prepared to invest time and attention to ensure a happy, healthy dog. When lifestyle compatibility, resources, and commitment align, the Cavapoo can become a beloved, lifelong companion, offering emotional support, joy, and unwavering affection.

Choosing a Cavapoo is a decision that goes beyond aesthetics or novelty. It is a commitment to nurturing a sensitive, intelligent, and loyal companion whose happiness depends on your engagement, care, and understanding. When chosen thoughtfully, the Cavapoo's presence enriches daily life, bringing love, companionship, and joy to households of all kinds.

Chapter 6

Choosing a Puppy or Adult Dog

Deciding to bring a Cavapoo into your home is only the first step. Equally important is determining whether to adopt or purchase, and if purchasing, selecting a responsible breeder. This chapter guides prospective owners through the considerations involved in choosing a Cavapoo puppy or adult dog, emphasizing health, temperament, and ethical practices. By understanding these factors, you can ensure a safe, fulfilling, and lifelong relationship with your new companion.

Adoption vs. Purchasing from a Breeder

Prospective owners face two primary avenues for acquiring a Cavapoo: adoption from a rescue organization or purchasing from a reputable breeder. Each option has advantages and considerations.

Adoption Advantages:

- **Saving a Life:** Many Cavapoos end up in rescues due to owner circumstances, health concerns, or unforeseen changes in lifestyle. Adopting a dog provides a second chance and directly helps animal welfare.
- **Cost Considerations:** Adoption fees are often lower than purchasing a puppy from a breeder. Fees typically include vaccinations, spaying or neutering, and basic health checks.
- **Behavioral Insight:** Rescue dogs may already exhibit stable behaviors, socialization, and training. Shelters often provide assessments of temperament and interactions with humans and other animals.
- **Supporting Ethical Practices:** Adoption discourages unethical breeding practices and contributes to responsible pet ownership culture.

Purchasing Advantages:

- **Predictable Traits:** Puppies from reputable breeders are more likely to display expected physical traits, temperament, and health characteristics. Breeders often specialize in maintaining specific coat types, sizes, and personality traits.

- **Health Clearances:** Ethical breeders conduct health screenings for common conditions in both parent breeds, reducing the likelihood of inherited disorders.
- **Early Socialization:** Puppies raised in attentive breeding programs often receive early socialization, helping them adapt to family life and training routines.
- **Lifetime Support:** Many responsible breeders provide guidance and support to new owners, assisting with behavioral or health questions long after the puppy leaves the breeder.

Both options require careful consideration. Prospective owners must assess their own ability to provide care, meet the dog's needs, and align their choice with ethical and responsible practices.

Evaluating Breeders

If purchasing from a breeder, it is essential to select one with ethical practices and a commitment to health and temperament.

The following criteria can help prospective owners evaluate breeders:

1. **Health** **Screenings:**
Responsible breeders perform comprehensive health checks on parent dogs to minimize the risk of hereditary issues. For Cavapoos, common health concerns to be screened include:

- Heart conditions (often inherited from Cavalier parents)
- Hip dysplasia and patellar luxation
- Eye conditions such as cataracts or retinal issues
- Allergies and skin sensitivities
  Request documentation of health clearances, including veterinary records and genetic testing reports.

2. **Temperament** **Testing:**
Ethical breeders assess the temperament of parent dogs to ensure puppies inherit stable, well-adjusted behavioral traits. Ask to meet the parent dogs to observe social behavior, friendliness, and interactions with humans and other animals.

3. **Breeding** **Practices:**
Reputable breeders follow responsible breeding guidelines, including:

- Limiting litters to ensure health and proper care of parent dogs
- Avoiding inbreeding to maintain genetic diversity
- Providing safe, clean, and enriched environments for puppies
- Early socialization through exposure to household sounds, children, and other pets

4. **Transparency** **and** **Communication:**
A trustworthy breeder welcomes questions, provides documentation, and maintains ongoing contact with puppy buyers. They should be willing to discuss health, lineage, grooming requirements, and temperament expectations without hesitation.

Red Flags to Watch For:

- Refusal to provide health records or meet parent dogs
- Multiple breeds offered in mass quantities

- Extremely low prices compared to standard market rates
- Lack of interest in the prospective owner's ability to provide care
- Puppies raised in poor conditions or isolated environments

Understanding Health Clearances

Health clearances are essential in reducing the likelihood of inherited diseases and ensuring long-term wellness. Prospective owners should seek documentation for both parent breeds, including tests such as:

- **Cardiac Screening:** Cavaliers are prone to mitral valve disease; Poodles can inherit heart conditions. Ensure parents have recent cardiac evaluations.
- **Hip and Joint Assessments:** Radiographs or evaluations for hip dysplasia and patellar luxation help predict potential orthopedic issues.
- **Eye Examinations:** Genetic eye testing is important for detecting cataracts, progressive retinal atrophy, or other inherited conditions.

- **Allergy and Skin Assessments:** Testing for sensitivities may help predict coat and skin conditions in puppies.

Health clearances provide peace of mind and reflect a breeder's commitment to ethical practices and long-term welfare.

Choosing an Adoption or Rescue Dog

For those considering adoption, evaluating a rescue dog's history, temperament, and health status is critical. Unlike puppies from breeders, rescue dogs may come with past experiences that influence behavior. Consider the following steps:

1. **Research Reputable Rescues:** Find organizations specializing in Cavapoos or small companion breeds. Look for rescues with good reputations for transparency, veterinary care, and post-adoption support.

2. **Assess Health and Vaccination Records:** Rescues should provide veterinary documentation, including vaccination history, spaying or neutering status, and any existing medical conditions.

3. Observe Behavior and Temperament: Many rescues conduct behavioral assessments to understand socialization levels, reactions to children, other pets, and new environments. Spend time with the dog before adoption to observe interactions, energy levels, and emotional responses.

4. Prepare for Adjustment: Rescue dogs may need time to acclimate to a new home. Patience, consistent training, and routine are essential to help the dog feel secure and build trust with new owners.

5. Advantages of Adoption:

- Opportunity to rescue a dog in need
- Usually lower cost than purchasing from breeders
- Often includes initial veterinary care, vaccinations, and spaying/neutering
- Supports ethical practices and discourages puppy mills

Selecting Between a Puppy and Adult Cavapoo

The decision to adopt or purchase a puppy versus an adult dog depends on lifestyle, experience, and household readiness:

Puppies:

- Require intensive training, socialization, and consistent care
- Allow owners to shape behaviors from an early age
- Provide the experience of raising a dog throughout its formative years
- Require patience with housebreaking, teething, and basic obedience

Adult Dogs:

- Often come partially or fully trained
- May have established temperament, making it easier to predict behavior
- Can be ideal for busy owners seeking a companion without intensive early training

- May require adjustment and patience if transitioning from a rescue environment

Both options can bring joy and fulfillment, but owners must understand the time, effort, and emotional commitment involved in each.

Preparing for Your Cavapoo

Regardless of whether you adopt or purchase, preparation is key to a successful transition:

1.   Home   Readiness:
Ensure your living space is safe, comfortable, and suitable for a small companion dog. Remove hazards, create cozy resting areas, and establish a designated space for feeding and play.

2.   Supplies:
Prepare essentials including food, water bowls, a comfortable bed, toys, grooming tools, leash, harness, and training aids.

3.   Veterinary   Connection:
Identify a veterinarian experienced with small breeds and

hybrid dogs. Schedule a wellness check soon after bringing your Cavapoo home.

4. Training Plan:
Develop a consistent routine for feeding, potty breaks, exercise, and training. Consider enrolling in puppy classes or obedience training to establish good habits early.

5. Emotional Preparation:
Cavapoos form strong attachments. Prepare to invest time, affection, and attention to ensure the dog feels secure and bonded to your family.

Ethical Considerations

Choosing a Cavapoo ethically means prioritizing the welfare of the dog and supporting responsible breeding or rescue practices. Avoid puppy mills, pet stores with poor conditions, and breeders who prioritize profit over health and temperament. Ethical choices ensure a healthier, happier companion and contribute to broader awareness of responsible pet ownership.

Conclusion

Choosing a Cavapoo, whether as a puppy or adult dog, is a decision that requires careful thought, research, and commitment. Adoption provides an opportunity to save a life and support ethical practices, while purchasing from a reputable breeder offers predictability in size, temperament, and health. Regardless of the path chosen, evaluating health clearances, temperament, and environmental compatibility is essential.

Prospective owners must consider lifestyle, time commitment, emotional readiness, and financial responsibility before making this important decision. A well-prepared home, thoughtful selection process, and commitment to care ensure that your Cavapoo thrives, forming a deep, lasting bond with you and your family. By approaching this decision responsibly, you set the foundation for a lifelong partnership filled with companionship, love, and joy.

Chapter 7

Preparing Your Home

Bringing a Cavapoo into your home is an exciting milestone, but careful preparation is essential to ensure a smooth transition. These intelligent and sensitive dogs thrive in environments that are safe, comfortable, and structured. Proper preparation reduces stress for both the dog and family members, sets the stage for effective training, and supports the dog's emotional and physical well-being. This chapter explores home preparation, puppy-proofing, essential supplies, and strategies for helping your Cavapoo adjust during the critical first days.

Understanding the Cavapoo's Needs

Cavapoos are affectionate, social, and intelligent dogs that form strong bonds with their owners. They require:

- **Safety:** A secure environment that prevents accidents or injury

- **Structure:** Consistent routines for feeding, potty breaks, and training
- **Stimulation:** Mental and physical engagement to prevent boredom and anxiety
- **Comfort:** Spaces to rest, relax, and feel secure

Home preparation begins with recognizing these needs and creating an environment that supports them.

Puppy-Proofing Your Home

Puppy-proofing is a crucial step before bringing a Cavapoo home. Even adult dogs benefit from a safe, well-organized space. Key areas of focus include:

1. Remove Hazards:

- Electrical cords should be secured or covered to prevent chewing and potential electrocution.
- Toxic plants, cleaning chemicals, medications, and human foods should be stored out of reach.
- Small objects such as coins, buttons, or toys that can be swallowed should be removed.

2. Secure Spaces:

- Use baby gates or closed doors to limit access to areas that are unsafe or off-limits.
- Ensure outdoor spaces are secure, with fences or gates that prevent escape.

3. Designate a Safe Zone:

- Create a designated area for the Cavapoo to rest and retreat.
- A crate or quiet corner with a bed provides a secure place where the dog can relax without disturbance.

4. Check Temperature and Comfort:

- Ensure rooms are well-ventilated and free from drafts or direct heat sources.
- Provide appropriate bedding and blankets to support comfort and security.

Essential Supplies

Having the right supplies on hand before your Cavapoo arrives ensures a smooth transition and supports early training. Essential items include:

Crate:

A crate provides a safe, comfortable space for your Cavapoo. It supports potty training, offers a retreat for rest, and creates a sense of security. Choose a crate that is appropriately sized, allowing the dog to stand, turn around, and lie down comfortably. Crate training should be gradual, using positive reinforcement to make the space inviting rather than punitive.

Bed:

A soft, supportive bed provides a dedicated resting area. Cavapoos appreciate cozy spaces, and having a bed in a quiet location encourages relaxation and a sense of ownership. Beds with washable covers are practical for maintaining hygiene, especially during the puppy stage.

Bowls:

- **Food and Water Bowls:** Stainless steel or ceramic bowls are preferred for durability and ease of cleaning. Avoid plastic bowls, which can harbor bacteria and cause allergic reactions in some dogs.
- **Placement:** Bowls should be placed in a consistent location, away from high-traffic areas, to support routine and comfort.

Toys:

- **Chew Toys:** Puppies and adult Cavapoos alike need safe chew toys to promote dental health and redirect natural chewing instincts.
- **Interactive Toys:** Puzzle toys, treat-dispensing toys, and other mentally stimulating items prevent boredom and support intelligence.
- **Soft Toys:** Gentle toys provide comfort and encourage interactive play, but should be monitored to prevent ingestion of loose parts.

Collar, Leash, and Harness:

- Select a properly fitting collar or harness that is comfortable and adjustable.
- A leash is essential for walks, training, and supervision in outdoor spaces.

Grooming Supplies:

- Brushes suitable for wavy, curly, or silky coats
- Nail clippers or grinders
- Dog-safe shampoo
- Ear cleaning solutions

Having these items ready ensures that the Cavapoo's basic needs are met from day one, supporting comfort, health, and safety.

Establishing Initial Routines

Cavapoos benefit from consistent routines that provide structure and predictability. Key routines to establish include:

Feeding:

- Determine a feeding schedule appropriate for age, size, and activity level. Puppies may require three to four meals per day, while adults typically eat twice daily.
- Measure portions according to nutritional guidelines to maintain healthy weight and prevent overeating.
- Maintain a quiet, consistent feeding area to reduce anxiety and reinforce routine.

Potty Training:

- Establish a designated potty area outside.
- Take the puppy or dog to this area consistently after waking, eating, drinking, and playtime.
- Positive reinforcement, such as treats and praise, encourages correct behavior.
- Be patient and consistent; accidents are normal during early training stages.

Exercise and Play:

- Schedule regular walks, short play sessions, and mental stimulation.

- Adjust exercise levels according to the dog's age, size, and energy level.
- Avoid overly strenuous activity for young puppies whose bones and joints are still developing.

Training and Socialization:

- Introduce basic commands such as sit, stay, and come using positive reinforcement.
- Gradually expose the dog to various environments, people, and animals to foster socialization.
- Avoid overwhelming the dog; short, frequent training sessions are more effective than long, exhausting ones.

First Days' Adjustment Strategies

The first days in a new home can be overwhelming for a Cavapoo. Thoughtful strategies reduce stress and promote a positive transition:

1. Gradual Introduction:

- Allow the dog to explore the home slowly, starting with a small, safe area.
- Introduce family members one at a time, minimizing overstimulation.

2. Establish Security:

- Encourage use of the crate or designated resting area for calm downtime.
- Avoid forcing interactions; let the dog approach people and new environments at its own pace.

3. Consistent Routine:

- Maintain predictable feeding, potty, and exercise schedules.
- Predictability reduces anxiety and supports learning.

4. Observation and Adjustment:

- Monitor behavior for signs of stress such as excessive whining, pacing, or withdrawal.
- Adjust the environment, routines, or interactions as needed to support comfort and confidence.

5. Positive Reinforcement:

- Reward desirable behaviors immediately with praise, treats, or play.
- Reinforce confidence, curiosity, and appropriate social interactions.

6. Limit Exposure to New Experiences:

- Gradually introduce new sounds, visitors, and household activities.
- Overexposure during the first days may overwhelm the dog, leading to anxiety or fear.

Preparing Family Members

Every household member should understand their role in welcoming the new Cavapoo:

- **Children:** Teach gentle handling, respecting the dog's space, and appropriate play.
- **Adults:** Coordinate responsibilities for feeding, exercise, grooming, and training.

- **Other Pets:** Introduce gradually, supervise interactions, and ensure safe spaces for all animals.

A collaborative approach ensures consistency and minimizes confusion for the dog, promoting smooth integration into family life.

Mental and Emotional Preparation

Prospective owners must be emotionally prepared for the responsibilities and challenges of a new Cavapoo:

- **Patience:** Puppies and newly adopted adults may test boundaries, require training, and make mistakes.
- **Flexibility:** Adjust routines as needed to accommodate the dog's personality and responses.
- **Commitment:** Recognize that establishing trust, confidence, and routine takes time and consistent effort.
- **Observation:** Pay attention to subtle cues indicating stress, illness, or discomfort. Early intervention improves outcomes and strengthens the bond.

Summary

Preparing your home for a Cavapoo involves more than providing supplies; it is about creating a safe, structured, and nurturing environment. Puppy-proofing, essential supplies, consistent routines, and careful observation all contribute to a successful transition. The first days are critical for reducing stress and anxiety, fostering confidence, and establishing the foundation for lifelong companionship.

By preparing thoughtfully, owners set their Cavapoo up for success, ensuring comfort, safety, and emotional security. This preparation reflects a commitment to responsible pet ownership and paves the way for a strong, lasting bond between dog and family. With proper planning, your home becomes a sanctuary for your Cavapoo—a place of comfort, joy, and shared adventure.

Chapter 8

Nutrition and Feeding

Nutrition is a cornerstone of a Cavapoo's health, growth, and longevity. Feeding the right diet, in appropriate quantities, and at the proper stages of life supports physical development, cognitive function, and overall well-being. This chapter provides a comprehensive guide to feeding Cavapoos at all life stages—puppy, adult, and senior—while addressing special considerations such as portion control, treats, supplements, obesity prevention, and sensitive stomachs. Proper nutrition is a lifelong commitment that plays a vital role in your Cavapoo's happiness and health.

Understanding the Cavapoo's Nutritional Needs

Cavapoos are a hybrid of the Cavalier King Charles Spaniel and Poodle, inheriting characteristics from both breeds. They are small to medium-sized dogs, generally weighing between 12 and 25 pounds, with moderate activity levels. Nutritional requirements are influenced by:

- **Age:** Puppies, adults, and seniors have differing caloric and nutrient needs.
- **Activity Level:** Active dogs require more calories, while less active dogs need fewer to maintain a healthy weight.
- **Size:** Smaller dogs, like Toy Cavapoos, may require more frequent meals to maintain stable energy levels.
- **Health Status:** Dogs with specific health concerns, allergies, or digestive sensitivities require tailored diets.

Balanced nutrition involves an appropriate combination of protein, fat, carbohydrates, fiber, vitamins, and minerals. High-quality commercial dog food or home-prepared meals under veterinary guidance can meet these requirements.

Feeding Puppies

Puppies have unique nutritional needs because they are rapidly growing and developing physically and mentally.

1. Protein Requirements:
High-quality protein supports muscle development, brain function, and overall growth. Look for foods where animal protein (chicken, beef, lamb, fish) is a primary ingredient.

2. Fat Content:
Healthy fats provide energy, support skin and coat health, and aid in absorption of fat-soluble vitamins. Omega-3 and Omega-6 fatty acids are particularly beneficial.

3. Meal Frequency:

- **Young Puppies (8–12 weeks):** Four meals per day to maintain stable energy and support digestion.
- **3–6 Months:** Three meals per day.
- **6–12 Months:** Transition to two meals per day.

4. Portion Control:
Follow guidelines provided on the dog food label, adjusted based on activity level, body condition, and growth rate. Overfeeding can lead to rapid weight gain and stress on developing joints, while underfeeding can stunt growth.

5. Hydration:

Ensure fresh, clean water is available at all times. Puppies are more susceptible to dehydration, particularly during play or warm weather.

6. Treats for Training:

Use small, low-calorie treats for training and positive reinforcement. Treats should not exceed 10% of the puppy's daily caloric intake to prevent overfeeding.

7. Special Considerations:

Puppies are prone to sensitive stomachs, particularly during dietary transitions. Introduce new foods gradually over 7–10 days, mixing increasing amounts of the new food with the old to prevent digestive upset.

Feeding Adult Cavapoos

Adult Cavapoos, typically between 1 and 7 years of age, require a balanced diet to maintain optimal weight, support energy needs, and promote overall health.

1. Protein and Fat:

- Adult dogs benefit from moderate protein levels to maintain lean muscle mass.
- Healthy fats remain important for energy, coat health, and cellular function.

2.   Carbohydrates   and   Fiber: Complex carbohydrates provide energy and support digestive health. Fiber aids in healthy bowel movements and promotes satiety.

3. Meal Frequency:

- Two meals per day is standard, typically morning and evening.
- Avoid free-feeding (leaving food out all day), which can contribute to overeating and weight gain.

4. Portion Control and Weight Monitoring:

- Adjust portion sizes based on activity levels, body condition, and age.
- Regularly assess weight, looking for a visible waistline and feeling for ribs without excessive fat covering.

5. Treats and Snacks:

- Use treats primarily for training or enrichment, keeping within recommended caloric limits.
- Opt for healthy options like small pieces of fruits or vegetables (carrots, green beans, apple slices without seeds).

6. Preventing Obesity:

- Cavapoos are prone to weight gain due to their love of food and small size.
- Regular exercise, appropriate portion sizes, and monitoring treats are key strategies to prevent obesity.
- Obesity can lead to joint stress, heart disease, and reduced life expectancy.

7. Special Dietary Needs:

- Some adult Cavapoos may develop sensitivities or food allergies, resulting in gastrointestinal upset, itching, or skin irritation.
- High-quality, limited-ingredient diets or veterinary-recommended formulas can alleviate these issues.

Feeding Senior Cavapoos

Senior Cavapoos, generally over 7 years of age, benefit from adjustments to diet that support aging joints, dental health, and overall vitality.

1. Adjusted Caloric Intake:

- Older dogs tend to be less active, so caloric intake should be reduced to prevent weight gain.
- Focus on nutrient-dense foods with lower calorie content.

2. Joint Health:

- Include foods or supplements containing glucosamine, chondroitin, and Omega-3 fatty acids to support joint function and mobility.

3. Digestive Health:

- Senior dogs may benefit from increased fiber to support gastrointestinal function and maintain regular bowel movements.

- Probiotics or easily digestible diets can be helpful for sensitive stomachs.

4. Protein and Muscle Maintenance:

- Adequate protein remains essential to preserve lean muscle mass and overall strength.
- High-quality, easily digestible protein sources are preferable.

5. Dental Care:

- Senior Cavapoos may have dental issues, making dry kibble or softer foods more manageable.
- Incorporate dental chews or specialized diets that support oral health.

Special Considerations for Sensitive Stomachs

Cavapoos, like many small breeds, can experience digestive sensitivities. Signs include vomiting, diarrhea, gas, or loose stools. Strategies for managing sensitive stomachs include:

- **Gradual Food Transitions:** Introduce new foods slowly over 7–10 days to prevent digestive upset.
- **High-Quality, Limited-Ingredient Diets:** Fewer ingredients reduce the likelihood of allergic reactions or intolerance.
- **Digestive Aids:** Probiotics, prebiotics, and fiber-rich foods support gut health.
- **Avoid Table Scraps:** Human foods, particularly fatty or spicy items, can upset sensitive stomachs.
- **Regular Feeding Schedule:** Consistency in meal times supports digestion and routine.

Supplements and Vitamins

While a balanced diet should meet most nutritional needs, some Cavapoos benefit from additional supplementation:

- **Omega-3 Fatty Acids:** Supports skin, coat, and joint health.
- **Glucosamine and Chondroitin:** Supports joint function, especially in active or senior dogs.

- **Probiotics:** Promotes digestive health and aids in nutrient absorption.
- **Multivitamins:** Only as recommended by a veterinarian to address specific deficiencies.

It is essential to consult a veterinarian before introducing supplements to ensure safety and prevent overdosing.

Hydration

Water is a critical component of nutrition. Ensure your Cavapoo has access to clean, fresh water at all times. Hydration supports digestion, circulation, temperature regulation, and overall health. Puppies, in particular, require frequent access to water to compensate for rapid growth and activity.

Feeding Tips for Success

1. **Consistent Schedule:** Feed at the same times each day to support routine and digestive health.
2. **Portion Control:** Measure food based on age, size, activity level, and caloric requirements.

3. **Monitor Weight:** Regularly assess body condition and adjust food intake accordingly.

4. **Limit Treats:** Keep treats under 10% of daily caloric intake to prevent weight gain.

5. **Observe Reactions:** Watch for signs of digestive upset or allergies and adjust diet as needed.

6. **Veterinary Guidance:** Consult a veterinarian for recommendations specific to age, health, or activity level.

Conclusion

Nutrition is a foundational component of Cavapoo care. Puppies require diets rich in protein and fat to support growth, adults need balanced nutrition to maintain health and prevent obesity, and seniors benefit from nutrient-dense, digestible foods to support aging joints and overall vitality. Special considerations for sensitive stomachs, treats, and supplements further enhance their well-being.

Feeding a Cavapoo is not merely a daily task—it is an ongoing commitment to their health, happiness, and longevity. By providing age-appropriate nutrition, monitoring portion sizes, and ensuring consistent routines, owners create a foundation for a healthy, active, and joyful life. Proper nutrition, coupled with exercise, training, and care, ensures that your Cavapoo thrives as a vibrant, loving companion for many years.

Chapter 9

Exercise and Mental Stimulation

Exercise and mental enrichment are essential components of Cavapoo care. These intelligent, affectionate, and energetic dogs thrive when their physical and cognitive needs are met. Proper exercise supports healthy weight, joint function, and cardiovascular health, while mental stimulation prevents boredom, reduces anxiety, and promotes behavioral stability. This chapter explores the daily exercise requirements, indoor and outdoor play, mental enrichment activities, and socialization strategies necessary to keep a Cavapoo healthy, happy, and well-adjusted.

Understanding the Cavapoo's Activity Needs

Cavapoos are hybrid dogs, inheriting traits from both the Cavalier King Charles Spaniel and the Poodle. This combination results in a breed that is:

- **Moderately Energetic:** Cavapoos enjoy play, short bursts of activity, and walks, but they do not require the high-intensity exercise of larger sporting breeds.
- **Intelligent:** Mental stimulation is just as important as physical exercise to prevent boredom-related behaviors such as chewing, digging, or excessive barking.
- **Social:** Cavapoos thrive on interaction with family members, other dogs, and their environment, making social play an effective form of enrichment.

Balancing physical and mental activity is essential for overall well-being.

Daily Exercise Requirements

A well-exercised Cavapoo is a happy Cavapoo. Exercise helps regulate energy levels, maintains healthy weight, supports joint and muscle health, and provides an outlet for natural behaviors.

1. Duration and Frequency:

- Puppies: Short, frequent sessions of 5–15 minutes several times per day are sufficient, as their developing bones and joints cannot handle extended, intense activity.
- Adults: 30–60 minutes of moderate exercise daily, split between walks, playtime, and interactive games.
- Seniors: Shorter, gentler walks and low-impact play, adapted to mobility and health considerations.

2. Types of Exercise:

- **Walks:** Regular walks provide physical activity, mental stimulation from exploring new scents and sights, and socialization opportunities.

- **Play Sessions:** Games such as fetch, tug-of-war, or chase in a safe, enclosed area meet both physical and mental needs.
- **Off-Leash Activity:** In secure environments or fenced yards, supervised off-leash time allows natural exploration, running, and interaction with family members or other dogs.

3.   Adjusting   Intensity: Activity levels should consider the dog's age, size, and health status. Puppies need careful monitoring to prevent overexertion, while adult Cavapoos benefit from consistent, structured exercise routines.

Indoor Play and Enrichment

Cavapoos adapt well to indoor environments, making indoor play a valuable tool for exercise, mental stimulation, and family interaction.

1. Interactive Play:

- Games like hide-and-seek, gentle tug-of-war, and chase around the house keep dogs physically active and engaged.
- Incorporating family members in play fosters bonding and social skills.

2. Training Games:

- Teach basic commands (sit, stay, come, heel) through short, rewarding sessions.
- Introduce new tricks to challenge cognitive skills, such as roll over, spin, or fetch specific items.
- Use positive reinforcement with treats or praise to encourage learning.

3. Puzzle Toys and Food Dispensers:

- Puzzle toys, treat balls, or slow feeders provide mental stimulation while rewarding problem-solving skills.
- These toys can be used to occupy dogs during alone time, reducing anxiety and destructive behavior.

4. Scent Games:

- Hide treats around the house for your Cavapoo to find using its keen sense of smell.
- Encourage problem-solving and exploration, satisfying natural instincts in a controlled environment.

Outdoor Exercise and Socialization

Outdoor activity allows Cavapoos to experience natural environments, develop social skills, and expend energy effectively.

1. Walks and Neighborhood Exploration:

- Walks provide low-impact aerobic exercise and exposure to different sights, sounds, and smells.
- Practice leash manners and reinforce basic commands during walks for both physical and mental stimulation.

2. Dog Parks and Playgroups:

- Supervised play with other dogs promotes socialization, communication skills, and healthy interaction.

- Gradually introduce new dogs to prevent stress or negative encounters.

3. Off-Leash Training:

- In secure, fenced areas, off-leash play allows Cavapoos to run freely, explore, and expend energy.
- Combine with recall training to ensure safety and control.

4. Outdoor Games:

- Fetch, frisbee, or agility-inspired exercises enhance coordination, fitness, and confidence.
- Adjust intensity according to age and physical ability, particularly for small or older Cavapoos.

Mental Enrichment Activities

Cavapoos' intelligence and curiosity require mental stimulation to prevent boredom-related behaviors. Mental enrichment can be incorporated alongside physical activity.

1. Obedience Training:

- Short, consistent sessions improve focus, communication, and behavior management.
- Reinforces owner-dog bond while challenging cognitive skills.

2. Trick Training:

- Advanced tricks, scent work, or agility exercises provide mental challenges and confidence-building.
- Use interactive rewards to maintain engagement.

3. Environmental Enrichment:

- Rotate toys to maintain novelty and prevent boredom.
- Provide safe objects for exploration and tactile engagement.
- Introduce new experiences gradually, such as car rides, visits to parks, or gentle exposure to new sounds.

4. Problem-Solving Games:

- Simple puzzles, treat retrieval games, or hide-and-seek exercises stimulate thinking and decision-making.

- Encourage independence while reinforcing positive behaviors.

Socialization as Mental Stimulation

Cavapoos are naturally social and benefit from structured socialization opportunities:

- **With People:** Interaction with family members, neighbors, and strangers in controlled settings develops confidence and reduces fear-based behaviors.
- **With Other Dogs:** Exposure to well-behaved, vaccinated dogs teaches appropriate play and communication skills.
- **With Environments:** Introduce new textures, sounds, and experiences to strengthen adaptability and reduce stress in unfamiliar situations.

Socialization should be positive, gradual, and consistent, providing enrichment while building confidence.

Balancing Exercise and Mental Stimulation

A balanced routine combines physical and cognitive activity:

- **Morning Walk:** Short, brisk walk for cardiovascular exercise and mental stimulation from outdoor exploration.
- **Midday Play or Training:** Indoor play session or puzzle toy engagement to challenge cognitive skills.
- **Evening Social Activity:** Gentle play, interaction with family, or supervised outdoor exploration to expend remaining energy.
- **Consistent Rest:** Ensure adequate downtime for recovery, particularly for puppies and senior dogs.

Balancing activity prevents overexertion, reduces stress, and maintains overall well-being.

Addressing Behavior Through Exercise and Enrichment

Insufficient exercise or mental stimulation can lead to undesirable behaviors:

- **Excessive Barking:** Often results from boredom or lack of engagement.
- **Chewing or Digging:** Redirect energy into appropriate toys and problem-solving games.
- **Separation Anxiety:** Mental enrichment and structured routines help alleviate stress during periods alone.
- **Hyperactivity:** Balanced physical activity and mental challenges moderate energy levels and improve focus.

Special Considerations

1. Puppies: Avoid high-impact or long-duration exercises to protect developing joints. Focus on short sessions and low-impact activities.

2. Senior Dogs: Adapt activities to mobility levels, provide gentle play, and prioritize mental engagement over physical exertion.

3. Health Issues: Monitor for signs of fatigue, lameness, or discomfort. Adjust intensity accordingly and consult a veterinarian for exercise restrictions due to health conditions.

4. Indoor Alternatives: In adverse weather or for apartment dwellers, create indoor obstacle courses, training games, or scent challenges to maintain stimulation.

Summary

Exercise and mental stimulation are integral to a Cavapoo's health and happiness. A combination of daily walks, play sessions, training games, puzzle toys, and socialization provides the physical and cognitive engagement these intelligent dogs need. Structured routines prevent behavioral issues, maintain healthy weight, and support emotional well-being.

Cavapoos thrive in households that balance activity, mental enrichment, and rest. Meeting their exercise and stimulation requirements fosters a confident, well-adjusted, and content companion. Thoughtful engagement strengthens the bond between owner and dog, ensuring a fulfilling and joyful relationship for both.

Chapter 10

Grooming and Coat Care

Grooming is a vital aspect of Cavapoo care, impacting not only appearance but also health, hygiene, and comfort. These small, hybrid dogs have coats that vary from wavy to curly, inherited from the Poodle parent, combined with the silky traits of the Cavalier King Charles Spaniel. Proper grooming prevents matting, maintains healthy skin and coat, and reduces the risk of infections or irritations. This chapter provides step-by-step instructions for brushing, bathing, trimming, ear cleaning, nail care, dental hygiene, and eye maintenance. It also outlines weekly, monthly, and seasonal grooming routines and guidance on professional versus home grooming.

Understanding the Cavapoo Coat

Cavapoos exhibit a range of coat types:

- **Curly:** Dense and highly textured, similar to a Poodle coat; tends to be low-shedding but requires regular maintenance to prevent mats.
- **Wavy:** A blend of soft waves and light curls; moderately low-shedding and easier to manage than a curly coat.
- **Silky/Straight:** More Cavalier influence; softer, fine hair that sheds more and may require frequent brushing to prevent tangles.

Coat type determines grooming needs, frequency, and tools required. Regular grooming is essential for all coat types to prevent discomfort, skin issues, and matting.

Brushing

Purpose: Brushing removes loose hair, dirt, and debris, prevents mats, and stimulates natural oils for a healthy, shiny coat.

Frequency:

- Curly: Daily or every other day to prevent tangles
- Wavy: 3–4 times per week

- Silky/Straight: 2–3 times per week, more often during shedding season

Tools Needed:

- Slicker brush for tangles and curls
- Pin brush for wavy coats
- Comb for sensitive areas and checking for mats
- Dematting tool for severe tangles

Step-by-Step Brushing:

1. Begin at the head and work towards the tail, brushing in sections.
2. Use gentle strokes to avoid pulling on hair.
3. Pay attention to behind ears, underarms, and tail, where mats often form.
4. Use a comb for sensitive areas or stubborn mats.
5. Reward your Cavapoo with praise or treats to create positive associations.

Bathing

Bathing maintains cleanliness, reduces odors, and supports skin health.

Frequency:

- Every 4–6 weeks for most Cavapoos
- More frequent baths if the dog becomes dirty or has a skin condition (consult a veterinarian)

Supplies Needed:

- Dog-safe shampoo and conditioner
- Towels and/or pet dryer
- Non-slip mat for safety

Bathing Steps:

1. Brush coat thoroughly before bathing to remove tangles.
2. Use lukewarm water and wet the coat completely.
3. Apply shampoo evenly, avoiding eyes and ears.
4. Gently massage the coat for proper cleansing.
5. Rinse thoroughly to remove all shampoo residue.

6. Apply conditioner if desired, especially for curly or wavy coats, and rinse.

7. Towel dry or use a pet-safe dryer on low heat, brushing gently while drying to prevent tangles.

Trimming and Haircuts

Cavapoos benefit from regular trimming to maintain a manageable coat, especially curly or wavy types.

Frequency:

- Every 6–10 weeks, depending on coat growth and lifestyle

Areas to Focus On:

- Face and muzzle for clear vision
- Around paws to prevent slipping and debris accumulation
- Sanitary areas to maintain hygiene
- Body coat for comfort and mat prevention

Tools:

- Grooming scissors for delicate areas
- Clippers for body trimming
- Comb and brush for finishing touches

Professional vs. Home Grooming:

- **Professional Grooming:** Ideal for first-time owners, curly coats, or intricate styles; ensures uniform trim and proper handling.
- **Home Grooming:** Suitable for owners comfortable with scissors, clippers, and brushing; regular maintenance between professional sessions is essential.

Ear Care

Cavapoos are prone to ear infections due to floppy ears that limit airflow.

Frequency:

- Weekly check and cleaning

Supplies Needed:

- Vet-approved ear cleaning solution
- Cotton balls or pads

Steps:

1. Gently lift the ear flap and inspect for redness, odor, or discharge.
2. Apply cleaning solution as directed.
3. Use a cotton ball to wipe the inner ear gently; avoid inserting deep into the canal.
4. Reward your dog for cooperation.

Nail Care

Regular nail trimming prevents discomfort, injury, and joint issues.

Frequency:

- Every 3–4 weeks, depending on growth and activity level

Supplies Needed:

- Dog nail clippers or grinder
- Styptic powder for emergencies

Steps:

1. Examine nails for length and health.
2. Trim small amounts gradually, avoiding the quick (the sensitive pink area with blood vessels).
3. Smooth edges with a grinder if desired.
4. Reward your dog to create positive associations with nail care.

Dental Care

Dental hygiene is crucial for Cavapoos, who are prone to tartar buildup and gum disease.

Frequency:

- Daily brushing is ideal
- Weekly or monthly professional dental checkups

Supplies:

- Dog toothbrush and toothpaste (never use human toothpaste)
- Dental chews or toys to supplement brushing

Steps:

1. Introduce toothbrush gradually with positive reinforcement.
2. Gently brush teeth in small, circular motions, focusing on gum lines.
3. Offer dental chews to support oral health.

Eye Care

Cavapoos may develop tear staining, particularly around light-colored coats.

Frequency:

- Daily check and cleaning as needed

Supplies:

- Soft, damp cloth or pet eye wipes

Steps:

1. Wipe around eyes gently to remove tear stains and debris.
2. Monitor for redness, discharge, or swelling; consult a veterinarian if persistent issues arise.

Weekly Grooming Schedule

- Brush coat according to type
- Check and clean ears
- Wipe eyes and monitor for staining
- Quick inspection of nails, teeth, and coat

Monthly Grooming Schedule

- Bathe and condition as needed
- Trim nails and hair around paws, face, and sanitary areas
- Inspect for fleas, ticks, or skin issues
- Introduce new grooming techniques gradually if performing home trims

Seasonal Grooming Considerations

- Spring/Summer: More frequent baths may be needed due to outdoor play and heat
- Fall/Winter: Coat may thicken; brushing frequency may increase to prevent mats
- Year-Round: Regular grooming prevents matting, reduces shedding, and supports overall health

Professional Grooming

Professional groomers provide expertise in trimming, styling, and handling, particularly for curly or high-maintenance coats. Benefits include:

- Even, hygienic trims
- Safe handling of anxious or squirmy dogs
- Expert attention to difficult areas such as paws, ears, and sanitary zones
- Guidance for maintaining a home grooming routine

Home Grooming

Home grooming is practical and cost-effective when performed regularly and safely. Key tips:

- Start early to acclimate puppies to brushes, baths, and clippers
- Keep sessions short, positive, and rewarding
- Use quality grooming tools appropriate for the dog's coat type
- Avoid rushing; consistency is more important than speed

Summary

Grooming is an essential aspect of Cavapoo care, promoting hygiene, comfort, and overall health. Brushing, bathing, trimming, ear cleaning, nail care, dental hygiene, and eye maintenance all contribute to a happy, well-cared-for dog. Establishing weekly, monthly, and seasonal routines ensures that grooming remains manageable and stress-free. Both professional and home grooming play valuable roles in maintaining the Cavapoo's coat and health.

By investing time and care into grooming, owners not only enhance their Cavapoo's appearance but also strengthen the human-animal bond, improve well-being, and prevent potential health issues. Grooming is more than a cosmetic activity—it is an expression of love, attention, and commitment to the dog's lifelong welfare.

Chapter 11

Training and Socialization

Training and socialization are fundamental aspects of Cavapoo ownership. These intelligent, affectionate, and sociable dogs thrive in environments where clear guidance, consistency, and positive reinforcement are applied. Proper training not only encourages desirable behaviors but also strengthens the bond between dog and owner, while socialization ensures confidence, adaptability, and emotional stability. This chapter provides a comprehensive guide to housebreaking, crate training, obedience commands, socialization with children and other pets, public exposure, and strategies for preventing separation anxiety and behavioral problems.

Understanding Cavapoo Intelligence and Temperament

Cavapoos inherit intelligence from the Poodle parent and the gentle, people-oriented temperament of the Cavalier King Charles Spaniel. These traits make them:

- **Quick Learners:** Capable of understanding commands and routines efficiently.
- **Sensitive:** Respond best to positive reinforcement rather than punishment.
- **Affectionate:** Thrive on attention and interaction, which can be leveraged during training.
- **Social:** Enjoy the company of people, children, and other animals, but need guided introductions.

Recognizing these characteristics allows owners to tailor training methods effectively.

Positive Reinforcement Training

Positive reinforcement is the most effective and humane training method for Cavapoos. It involves rewarding desired behaviors to encourage repetition.

Key Principles:

1. **Consistency:** Use the same commands, cues, and rewards to avoid confusion.
2. **Timing:** Reward immediately after the desired behavior to reinforce learning.
3. **Motivation:** Use treats, praise, toys, or play as rewards, depending on what motivates your dog most.
4. **Short Sessions:** Keep training sessions 5–15 minutes for puppies and 15–20 minutes for adults to maintain focus.
5. **Patience:** Learning is a process; avoid frustration or punishment, which can lead to anxiety or fear.

Housebreaking and Potty Training

Housebreaking is often the first priority for new Cavapoo owners. Early consistency and routine are key to successful potty training.

Steps for Housebreaking:

1. **Establish a Schedule:** Take the puppy outside after waking, eating, drinking, playing, and before bedtime.
2. **Designate a Potty Area:** Choose a consistent location to encourage recognition and routine.
3. **Use Commands:** Simple cues like "go potty" help the dog associate the action with the verbal command.
4. **Supervise and Confine:** Limit unsupervised access indoors using baby gates or a crate.
5. **Reward Success:** Immediately praise, offer treats, or engage in play to reinforce correct behavior.
6. **Handle Accidents Calmly:** Avoid punishment; clean thoroughly to remove odors and prevent repeat incidents.

Crate Training

Crate training provides a safe, comfortable space for the Cavapoo and supports housebreaking, routine, and stress reduction.

Steps for Crate Training:

1. **Introduce Gradually:** Allow the dog to explore the crate voluntarily. Place treats or toys inside to encourage entry.
2. **Short Sessions:** Begin with brief periods and gradually increase duration as comfort grows.
3. **Positive Association:** Feed meals inside the crate and offer rewards for calm behavior.
4. **Avoid Using as Punishment:** The crate should be a sanctuary, not a place of discipline.
5. **Consistency:** Incorporate crate time into daily routines to foster security and predictability.

Basic Obedience Commands

Cavapoos respond well to structured obedience training, which promotes safety, control, and communication.

Essential Commands:

1. **Sit:** Foundation for polite behavior and control in various situations.
2. **Stay:** Teaches patience and self-control.
3. **Come:** Essential for recall and safety outdoors.
4. **Heel:** Promotes proper leash walking and reduces pulling.
5. **Leave It / Drop It:** Prevents ingestion of harmful items and reinforces impulse control.
6. **Down:** Encourages calm behavior and reduces hyperactivity.

Training Tips:

- Use treats, praise, and play consistently.
- Train in quiet, low-distraction environments initially.

- Gradually increase distractions to generalize behavior in real-world settings.

Socialization with Children and Family Members

Cavapoos are naturally gentle and affectionate but require proper introductions to children and family members to prevent stress or misunderstandings.

Steps for Successful Socialization:

1. **Supervised Interactions:** Monitor interactions with young children to ensure gentle handling.
2. **Teach Respect:** Educate children on appropriate ways to pet, play, and approach the dog.
3. **Gradual Exposure:** Introduce the dog to extended family members or visitors slowly.
4. **Positive Experiences:** Reward calm, friendly behavior during interactions.

Socialization with Other Pets

Early and positive introductions to other dogs, cats, or household animals prevent fear or aggression.

Techniques:

- Use neutral territory for initial meetings to avoid territorial behavior.
- Keep initial encounters short and controlled.
- Observe body language and separate animals if tension arises.
- Reward positive interactions and gradually extend playtime.

Public Exposure and Community Socialization

Cavapoos benefit from exposure to public spaces, sights, sounds, and people, which reduces fear and promotes confidence.

Approach:

1. **Start Gradually:** Begin with short trips to low-traffic areas.
2. **Positive Reinforcement:** Reward calm and confident behavior with treats or praise.
3. **Variety of Experiences:** Introduce parks, sidewalks, pet-friendly stores, and outdoor cafes.
4. **Monitor Stress Levels:** Avoid overwhelming environments initially; build confidence slowly.

Preventing Separation Anxiety

Cavapoos form strong attachments to their owners, which can lead to separation anxiety if not managed properly. Signs include whining, destructive behavior, or excessive barking when left alone.

Strategies to Prevent or Mitigate Anxiety:

1. **Gradual Alone Time:** Start with short periods and gradually increase duration.

2. **Safe Environment:** Ensure the dog has access to a comfortable space with toys, water, and a crate if trained.

3. **Mental and Physical Stimulation:** Exercise and enrichment before departure reduce excess energy and stress.

4. **Consistent Departure Cues:** Avoid dramatic exits; maintain calm, routine behaviors when leaving and returning.

5. **Professional Guidance:** Severe cases may benefit from veterinary advice, behavioral training, or pheromone therapies.

Addressing Behavior Problems

Early intervention is critical to prevent or correct undesirable behaviors. Common issues include:

- **Excessive Barking:** Often caused by boredom, anxiety, or attention-seeking; addressed with mental stimulation and consistent boundaries.
- **Chewing or Destructive Behavior:** Provide appropriate chew toys and redirect attention.

- **Jumping on People:** Train "sit" or "off" commands and reward calm greetings.
- **Leash Pulling:** Use proper leash training techniques and rewards for walking politely.

Consistency, patience, and positive reinforcement are key to managing and preventing behavior problems.

Training Tips for Success

- **Short, Frequent Sessions:** 5–15 minutes multiple times a day is more effective than long, exhausting sessions.
- **Positive Environment:** Avoid punishment; use treats, praise, and play as motivation.
- **Patience and Consistency:** Progress may be gradual, particularly with sensitive or shy dogs.
- **Observation:** Monitor stress, fatigue, or frustration and adjust training intensity accordingly.
- **Enrichment Integration:** Combine training with mental stimulation activities such as puzzle toys, scent work, or interactive games.

Summary

Training and socialization are essential for raising a well-adjusted, confident, and happy Cavapoo. Positive reinforcement, consistent routines, and early socialization with children, other pets, and public environments foster good behavior and emotional stability. Housebreaking, crate training, obedience commands, and mental enrichment lay the foundation for a lifetime of companionship and trust. Preventing separation anxiety and addressing behavioral challenges proactively ensures that your Cavapoo thrives in any environment.

By investing time and effort in training and socialization, owners cultivate a dog that is not only obedient and well-behaved but also confident, secure, and socially adept. Training is an ongoing journey that deepens the bond between dog and owner, creating a rewarding, lifelong partnership built on understanding, respect, and love.

Chapter 12

Health, Veterinary Care, and Lifespan

Caring for a Cavapoo's health is essential for ensuring a long, happy, and fulfilling life. As a hybrid of the Cavalier King Charles Spaniel and the Poodle, Cavapoos inherit a combination of traits that influence their overall health, susceptibility to certain conditions, and lifespan. Preventive care, early detection of medical issues, and consistent veterinary guidance are critical for maintaining vitality. This chapter explores common health concerns, preventive strategies, vaccination schedules, the importance of routine veterinary care, and considerations for lifespan and aging.

Understanding Cavapoo Health

Cavapoos are generally healthy dogs, but hybrid genetics do not completely eliminate the risk of inherited conditions from either parent breed. Understanding potential health issues and implementing proactive care measures allows owners to mitigate risks and ensure early treatment if problems arise.

Common Health Concerns

Heart Disease

Cavapoos can inherit predispositions to heart disease, primarily from the Cavalier King Charles Spaniel lineage.

- **Mitral Valve Disease (MVD):** A common cardiac condition in Cavaliers that may be passed to Cavapoos. MVD involves the degeneration of the mitral valve, leading to heart murmurs, coughing, fatigue, and, in severe cases, heart failure.
- **Prevention and Monitoring:** Regular veterinary check-ups, auscultation, and echocardiograms for high-risk dogs help detect early signs. Maintaining a healthy weight and avoiding overexertion can support cardiac health.

Joint Issues

Joint problems can affect mobility and quality of life. Cavapoos may inherit tendencies toward:

- **Patellar Luxation:** Kneecap dislocation causing pain and lameness.
- **Hip Dysplasia:** Malformation of the hip joint leading to arthritis or discomfort.
- **Preventive Measures:** Maintain healthy body weight, provide joint-supportive supplements (like glucosamine and chondroitin), and avoid high-impact exercise in young puppies. Early veterinary evaluation can guide management or intervention.

Eye Problems

Eye health is important due to the Cavalier parent's susceptibility to conditions such as:

- **Cataracts:** Clouding of the lens, potentially affecting vision.
- **Progressive Retinal Atrophy (PRA):** Degenerative condition that can lead to blindness.

- **Dry Eye (Keratoconjunctivitis Sicca):** Insufficient tear production causing irritation.
- **Prevention and Care:** Regular eye checks, cleaning discharge around the eyes, and prompt veterinary attention for redness, cloudiness, or excessive tearing.

Ear Infections

Cavapoos have floppy ears, which can trap moisture and debris, creating an environment prone to infection.

- **Signs:** Scratching, redness, odor, or discharge from the ear canal.
- **Prevention:** Weekly ear checks and cleaning with veterinarian-approved solutions. Dry ears thoroughly after baths or swimming.

Dental Health

Small breeds, including Cavapoos, are prone to dental issues such as tartar buildup, gingivitis, and periodontal disease.

- **Prevention:** Daily brushing with dog-safe toothpaste, dental chews, and regular veterinary dental exams.

- **Early Signs:** Bad breath, difficulty chewing, or swollen gums should prompt immediate attention.

Preventive Care

Preventive care is the foundation of a long, healthy life for a Cavapoo. Key components include:

- **Routine Veterinary Check-Ups:** Annual or biannual visits to monitor health, administer vaccines, and assess growth and weight. Puppies require more frequent visits in their first year.
- **Vaccinations:** Core vaccines typically include:
  - Distemper
  - Parvovirus
  - Adenovirus
  - Rabies

    Optional vaccines may include Bordetella (kennel cough), Leptospirosis, and Lyme disease, depending on lifestyle and geographic location.
- **Parasite Prevention:** Regular flea, tick, and heartworm prevention, as recommended by a veterinarian.

- **Nutrition and Weight Management:** Balanced diet, portion control, and avoiding obesity reduce the risk of joint, heart, and metabolic conditions.
- **Exercise and Mental Enrichment:** Moderate physical activity and cognitive engagement support cardiovascular, joint, and mental health.
- **Grooming and Hygiene:** Regular brushing, bathing, nail care, ear cleaning, and dental hygiene prevent infections, mats, and related complications.

Routine Health Monitoring

Owners should be proactive in observing changes that could indicate health concerns:

- Appetite or weight fluctuations
- Lethargy or changes in activity level
- Vomiting, diarrhea, or gastrointestinal issues
- Coughing, sneezing, or labored breathing
- Changes in coat, skin, or coat shedding
- Behavioral changes or signs of pain

Prompt veterinary attention ensures early diagnosis and treatment, significantly improving outcomes.

Lifespan and Aging Care

Cavapoos typically live between 12 and 15 years, with proper care. Lifespan and quality of life are influenced by genetics, nutrition, exercise, preventive care, and prompt management of health issues.

Senior Dog Considerations:

- **Diet Adjustments:** Seniors may benefit from lower-calorie, nutrient-dense diets to prevent obesity while supporting joint health.
- **Joint Support:** Incorporate supplements like glucosamine, chondroitin, and Omega-3 fatty acids.
- **Dental Care:** Seniors are more prone to tartar buildup and tooth loss; maintain regular brushing and checkups.
- **Regular Veterinary Assessments:** Increase frequency of exams to monitor age-related changes in heart, kidneys, liver, and mobility.

- **Comfort and Accessibility:** Provide orthopedic beds, easy access to food, water, and outdoor areas, and gentle exercise routines.

Genetic Testing and Responsible Breeding

Responsible breeders perform genetic testing to minimize the risk of inherited health issues. Before acquiring a Cavapoo, ensure breeders provide:

- Health clearances for both parent breeds
- Veterinary records and vaccination history
- Transparent discussion of potential genetic risks

Genetic testing helps owners anticipate possible concerns and take preventive measures early.

Emergency Preparedness

Even with preventive care, emergencies can occur. Owners should be prepared to:

- Recognize symptoms of distress (difficulty breathing, severe pain, collapse)
- Contact an emergency veterinary clinic immediately
- Maintain a first-aid kit, including bandages, styptic powder, and pet-safe antiseptic
- Know the location of nearby 24-hour veterinary services

Supporting a Healthy Lifestyle

Beyond veterinary care, daily practices support longevity:

- **Consistent Exercise:** Maintain mobility, cardiovascular health, and weight management.
- **Balanced Nutrition:** Age-appropriate diets for puppies, adults, and seniors.
- **Mental Stimulation:** Puzzle toys, training, and social interaction prevent cognitive decline and behavioral issues.
- **Social Engagement:** Regular interaction with family, friends, and other pets improves emotional well-being.
- **Grooming:** Prevents skin infections, maintains coat health, and allows early detection of abnormalities.

Summary

Caring for a Cavapoo's health involves proactive, preventive strategies, consistent veterinary oversight, and daily attentiveness to physical and emotional well-being. Common health concerns, including heart disease, joint issues, eye problems, ear infections, and dental disease, require monitoring and early intervention. Vaccination, parasite prevention, nutrition, exercise, grooming, and mental stimulation all contribute to a long and fulfilling life. With proper care, Cavapoos typically live 12–15 years, enjoying vitality, companionship, and family integration well into their senior years.

Owners who prioritize health, establish routines, and maintain regular communication with their veterinarian provide the foundation for a lifetime of happiness and comfort for their Cavapoo. Vigilance, proactive care, and a commitment to quality of life transform pet ownership into a deeply rewarding, lifelong journey.

Chapter 13

Traveling and Lifestyle Adaptations

Cavapoos are affectionate, adaptable, and social dogs that thrive when included in family life. However, travel and lifestyle changes can present challenges for both the dog and the owner. Ensuring safe transportation, maintaining routines, and accommodating a Cavapoo's needs in various settings are essential for their well-being. This chapter provides comprehensive guidance on safe travel, crate training for cars, air travel considerations, pet-friendly accommodations, boarding options, and lifestyle adjustments for working owners.

Understanding the Cavapoo's Adaptability

Cavapoos are intelligent and social, inheriting traits from the Cavalier King Charles Spaniel and Poodle. Their adaptability makes them good companions for:

- Families with children
- Seniors seeking companionship
- Owners with active or busy lifestyles

However, their attachment to humans and sensitivity can cause stress in unfamiliar environments. Preparing for travel and lifestyle changes reduces anxiety and ensures a safe, enjoyable experience.

Safe Travel by Car

Car travel is a common scenario for Cavapoo owners, whether for errands, vacations, or veterinary visits. Safety and comfort are paramount.

Crate Training for Cars:

- **Purpose:** Prevents distraction to the driver, reduces injury risk in accidents, and provides a secure, familiar environment.
- **Crate Selection:** Use a sturdy, well-ventilated crate that fits the dog comfortably. Ensure it can be secured with seat belts or straps.
- **Familiarization:** Introduce the crate at home with treats, toys, and bedding. Gradually increase time spent inside to create positive associations.
- **Travel Tips:**
  1. Take short trips first to acclimate your Cavapoo.
  2. Bring water and a collapsible bowl for longer trips.
  3. Avoid feeding large meals immediately before travel to reduce motion sickness.
  4. Make regular stops on longer journeys for bathroom breaks and exercise.

Harness and Seatbelt Options:

- For dogs that resist crates, a well-fitted harness with a seatbelt attachment provides safety and restraint.
- Ensure the harness does not allow excessive movement or sliding in the vehicle.

Air Travel Considerations

Air travel presents unique challenges for small dogs like Cavapoos, particularly due to temperature, pressure, and stress factors.

Cabin vs. Cargo:

- **Cabin Travel:** Preferred for small breeds under 20 pounds. Dogs remain with owners in an airline-approved carrier under the seat.
- **Cargo Travel:** Less desirable due to separation and stress; only recommended when cabin travel is unavailable.

Carrier Requirements:

- Airline-approved soft or hard-sided carriers that allow standing, turning, and lying down.
- Adequate ventilation and secure closures.
- Familiar bedding or toys to provide comfort and reduce anxiety.

Preparation Steps:

1. **Vet Check:** Ensure the Cavapoo is healthy for travel and up-to-date on vaccinations.
2. **Acclimation:** Introduce the carrier at home and encourage the dog to spend time inside with positive reinforcement.
3. **Hydration and Bathroom Needs:** Offer water and a chance to relieve themselves before boarding.
4. **Documentation:** Carry vaccination records, identification, and health certificates as required by airlines.

Pet-Friendly Accommodations

Traveling with a Cavapoo often involves overnight stays in hotels, rentals, or vacation homes. Selecting pet-friendly accommodations ensures a safe and comfortable experience.

Considerations:

- Confirm pet policies, fees, and size restrictions.
- Check for secure outdoor spaces for bathroom breaks.
- Look for accommodations near walking areas or parks.
- Bring familiar bedding, toys, and feeding supplies to maintain routine.

Behavioral Expectations:

- Cavapoos thrive on routine, so maintain consistent feeding, potty, and exercise schedules.
- Supervise interactions in shared spaces and public areas to prevent stress or accidents.

Boarding and Daycare

For owners with work commitments or extended travel, boarding or doggy daycare may be necessary. Proper selection ensures safety, comfort, and socialization.

Boarding Options:

- **Professional Kennels:** Offer structured care, supervision, and often grooming and exercise.
- **Pet Sitters:** In-home care provides individualized attention and comfort in a familiar environment.
- **Family or Friends:** Trusted individuals may provide care if familiar with the dog's routine and needs.

Preparation:

1. Provide clear instructions for feeding, exercise, medication, and routines.
2. Supply familiar bedding, toys, and comfort items.
3. Introduce the Cavapoo to the environment before extended stays when possible.

Lifestyle Adjustments for Working Owners

Owners with full-time jobs must ensure that Cavapoos receive adequate care, attention, and stimulation despite a busy schedule.

Daily Routine Considerations:

- **Morning Exercise:** Short walk or play session to expend energy before leaving for work.
- **Mental Stimulation:** Puzzle toys, treat-dispensing toys, or safe chews to occupy the dog during absence.
- **Bathroom Breaks:** Arrange for a dog walker, neighbor, or daycare to prevent accidents and provide relief.
- **Evening Bonding:** Exercise, play, training, and affection after returning home maintain emotional health and strengthen the human-animal bond.

Tips for Success:

- Maintain consistent feeding, walking, and bedtime routines.

- Avoid sudden changes in schedule, as Cavapoos thrive on predictability.
- Incorporate socialization opportunities, even brief, to prevent isolation or anxiety.
- Observe the dog's behavior for signs of stress, such as excessive barking, chewing, or withdrawal, and adjust routines accordingly.

Travel Preparation Checklist

To ensure smooth travel experiences:

- **Health:** Vet check, vaccinations, and documentation.
- **Comfort:** Crate, bedding, and familiar toys.
- **Safety:** Harness, seatbelt, or carrier secured in vehicle.
- **Supplies:** Food, water, bowls, cleanup materials, medications, and first-aid kit.
- **Routine:** Maintain feeding, bathroom, and exercise schedule as closely as possible.
- **Behavior:** Practice short trips to acclimate the dog and reduce stress.

Encouraging Positive Travel Experiences

Creating positive associations with travel reduces anxiety:

- Praise and reward calm behavior during preparation, transport, and arrival.
- Avoid forcing the dog into carriers or vehicles abruptly.
- Gradually expose the dog to travel routines, starting with short, low-stress trips.
- Reinforce travel as a fun experience with treats, walks, and play at destinations.

Summary

Traveling with a Cavapoo and adapting lifestyle routines requires planning, preparation, and consideration of the dog's physical, emotional, and social needs. Safe car travel, air travel readiness, pet-friendly accommodations, boarding options, and structured daily routines support the well-being of working owners and their dogs. By maintaining consistency, providing mental and physical stimulation, and creating positive associations, Cavapoos can enjoy travel, new environments, and changes in daily life while remaining happy, healthy, and well-adjusted.

Chapter 14

Enrichment, Bonding, and Emotional Health

Cavapoos are not only intelligent and playful but also deeply social and emotionally sensitive dogs. Their hybrid lineage, combining the gentle, affectionate Cavalier King Charles Spaniel with the intelligent, trainable Poodle, gives them a unique blend of cognitive ability and emotional awareness. This combination makes Cavapoos excellent companions, therapy animals, and family pets. Beyond basic care, these dogs require mental stimulation, emotional engagement, and meaningful bonding activities to flourish. This chapter explores strategies for enrichment, bonding, interactive games, therapy and companion roles, and managing stress during household changes.

Understanding Emotional Needs

Cavapoos thrive in environments where their emotional and social needs are met. Unmet needs can lead to behavioral issues, stress, or anxiety. Understanding their emotional landscape allows owners to provide supportive care:

- **Attachment:** Cavapoos form strong bonds with their owners and family members.
- **Sensitivity:** They respond to tone, body language, and mood, making gentle, consistent interaction important.
- **Curiosity:** Their intelligence drives them to explore and solve problems, requiring mental challenges to prevent boredom.
- **Social Orientation:** Interaction with humans, other pets, and varied environments enriches their emotional well-being.

Owners who recognize and honor these emotional traits can create a supportive, stimulating, and balanced life for their Cavapoo.

Mental Enrichment Activities

Mental stimulation is as critical as physical exercise for Cavapoos. Enrichment activities challenge the mind, prevent boredom, and strengthen cognitive skills.

1. Puzzle Toys and Treat Dispensers:

- Encourage problem-solving and persistence.
- Vary difficulty levels as the dog becomes more adept.
- Use food or small toys as rewards to sustain interest.

2. Scent Work:

- Hide treats around the home or yard for scent-tracking exercises.
- Scent games stimulate natural instincts and enhance focus.
- Advanced scent challenges, such as hiding a specific scent for the dog to locate, improve problem-solving skills.

3. Trick Training:

- Teach new tricks such as roll over, spin, fetch specific items, or agility exercises.
- Combine physical movement with mental challenge for holistic stimulation.
- Keep sessions short and rewarding to maintain motivation.

4. Interactive Games:

- Tug-of-war, hide-and-seek, and fetch variations provide engagement and mental challenges.
- Modify games to suit indoor or outdoor environments while maintaining safety.

Bonding Activities

Strong bonds between owner and dog improve trust, obedience, and emotional security. Cavapoos, being highly social, benefit from consistent interaction and shared activities.

1. Structured Play:

- Incorporate both physical activity and cognitive challenges.
- Use toys, puzzles, or obstacle courses to engage multiple senses.

2. Training Sessions:

- Positive reinforcement training strengthens communication and understanding.
- Regular sessions reinforce trust, respect, and predictability in daily life.

3. Routine Shared Activities:

- Daily walks, family outings, or quiet time together promote attachment.
- Consistent routines provide stability, reducing anxiety during changes.

4. Gentle Massage and Touch:

- Massage and petting provide relaxation, strengthen bonds, and support emotional well-being.

- Focus on pressure points, ears, shoulders, and back for comfort and trust-building.

Therapy and Companion Roles

Cavapoos' affectionate temperament and intelligence make them excellent therapy and companion animals. Engaging them in these roles provides purpose, socialization, and mental engagement.

1. Therapy Work:

- Visits to hospitals, nursing homes, or schools provide social interaction and emotional support.
- Training for therapy roles enhances obedience, patience, and resilience.
- Positive experiences reinforce confidence and social skills.

2. Companion Roles:

- Emotional support for family members, seniors, or children.

- Interaction during daily routines encourages routine adherence and reduces loneliness.
- Encourage gentle, supportive behavior through calm, structured interaction.

Building Trust

Trust is essential for a Cavapoo's emotional health. A secure dog is confident, well-behaved, and adaptable to new environments.

Strategies to Build Trust:

- Respond consistently to behavior with predictable outcomes.
- Avoid punishment; redirect undesirable behavior calmly.
- Provide safe spaces such as a crate or designated area where the dog can relax.
- Offer choices during play or training to empower the dog and enhance confidence.

Coping with Stress and Household Changes

Cavapoos may experience stress due to:

- Changes in routine (work schedules, moving, or renovations)
- Introduction of new family members or pets
- Travel, boarding, or veterinary visits
- Loud noises or unfamiliar environments

Managing Stress:

1. **Predictable Routines:** Maintain feeding, exercise, and bonding schedules.
2. **Gradual Introductions:** Introduce new people, pets, or environments slowly and positively.
3. **Safe Spaces:** Provide quiet areas for retreat and relaxation.
4. **Mental and Physical Engagement:** Active enrichment reduces anxiety and boredom.

5. **Observation:** Monitor behavior for signs of stress such as pacing, whining, hiding, or excessive licking.

Encouraging Positive Socialization

Ongoing socialization prevents fear, aggression, and anxiety:

- **Human Interaction:** Regular contact with diverse people, including children and seniors, promotes confidence.
- **Pet Interaction:** Supervised play with dogs and other animals develops communication skills.
- **Environmental Exposure:** Exposure to varied environments, sounds, and textures reduces fearfulness and builds adaptability.

Advanced Enrichment Strategies

For well-established Cavapoos, advanced enrichment challenges cognitive and physical abilities:

1. **Agility Courses:** Mini obstacle courses in the yard or home improve coordination and focus.

2. **Scent Discrimination Games:** Teach the dog to identify and retrieve specific scents.

3. **Interactive Technology:** Automated treat dispensers, puzzle feeders, and training apps provide mental stimulation during owner absence.

4. **Problem-Solving Tasks:** Encourage independent thinking, such as opening boxes or finding hidden toys.

Integrating Enrichment into Daily Life

Daily routines provide opportunities for enrichment:

- Morning walks combined with scent exploration and obedience practice.
- Midday interactive play or training sessions for mental engagement.
- Evening calm bonding activities like massage, gentle play, or puzzle toys.
- Incorporate enrichment seamlessly with feeding, potty breaks, and social interactions.

Emotional Health and Lifelong Engagement

Maintaining emotional well-being is a lifelong process. Owners should:

- Observe mood and behavior for early signs of distress or depression.
- Provide consistent affection and engagement without overstimulation.
- Adapt routines during aging or health changes to accommodate energy and mobility.
- Encourage confidence through positive reinforcement and safe exploration.
- Use bonding and enrichment to mitigate separation anxiety, boredom, or behavioral challenges.

Summary

Cavapoos thrive when their minds and hearts are actively engaged. Enrichment activities, bonding routines, interactive games, therapy roles, and socialization all contribute to a well-rounded, emotionally healthy dog. Building trust, providing consistent routines, and offering challenges that stimulate intelligence support resilience, adaptability, and confidence. By integrating mental, physical, and emotional enrichment into daily life, owners foster a lifelong bond that promotes happiness, security, and mutual fulfillment. Cavapoos are more than pets—they are companions whose emotional and cognitive needs are as important as their physical care.

Chapter 15

Responsible Ownership and Lifelong Commitment

Owning a Cavapoo is a journey of love, devotion, and responsibility. These intelligent, affectionate, and social dogs bring joy, companionship, and emotional enrichment to family life, but they also require thoughtful planning, consistent care, and long-term commitment. A Cavapoo's well-being depends on the owner's dedication to physical health, mental stimulation, socialization, financial preparedness, and ethical responsibility. This final chapter serves as a comprehensive guide to lifelong Cavapoo ownership, emphasizing the rewards, responsibilities, and ethical considerations of caring for these remarkable companions.

Understanding the Lifelong Commitment

Cavapoos typically live between 12 and 15 years, and some may surpass this range with optimal care. Their longevity demands consistent attention to daily routines, health monitoring, and emotional support. Owners must understand that a Cavapoo is not a temporary companion or a casual indulgence; it is a lifelong responsibility that requires time, patience, and love.

Key Elements of Lifelong Commitment:

- **Daily Care:** Regular feeding, exercise, grooming, and training.
- **Health Maintenance:** Routine veterinary checkups, vaccinations, dental care, and preventive treatments.
- **Mental and Emotional Engagement:** Enrichment, bonding, and socialization throughout the dog's life.
- **Adaptability:** Adjusting care as the dog ages, faces health challenges, or encounters lifestyle changes.
- **Financial Planning:** Budgeting for food, medical care, grooming, training, and unexpected emergencies.

Ethical and Responsible Ownership

Owning a Cavapoo carries ethical responsibilities that extend beyond meeting basic needs. Responsible ownership ensures the dog's physical and emotional well-being while promoting humane treatment and societal responsibility.

Principles of Ethical Ownership:

1. **Commitment to Welfare:** Providing adequate nutrition, exercise, grooming, and healthcare throughout the dog's life.

2. **Avoiding Impulse Acquisition:** Careful research before acquiring a Cavapoo ensures compatibility with lifestyle, living space, and resources.

3. **Supporting Ethical Breeding and Adoption:** Choosing responsible breeders or reputable rescue organizations helps reduce genetic health problems and discourages puppy mills.

4. **Preventing Neglect or Abandonment:** Understanding the long-term commitment minimizes the risk of surrendering the dog due to unforeseen circumstances.

5. **Advocacy and Education:** Promoting responsible pet ownership, socialization, and community awareness about Cavapoos and hybrid breeds.

Financial Planning for a Cavapoo

Caring for a Cavapoo involves predictable and unexpected expenses. Financial preparedness ensures consistent quality of life and reduces stress for both owner and pet.

Estimated Financial Considerations:

- **Initial Costs:** Purchase price or adoption fees, spaying/neutering, vaccinations, initial supplies (crate, bed, bowls, toys, grooming tools).
- **Routine Expenses:** Food, treats, grooming, preventive veterinary care, flea/tick/heartworm prevention, and routine checkups.
- **Training and Enrichment:** Professional training, classes, and enrichment toys or equipment.
- **Emergency Medical Care:** Unexpected illnesses, accidents, or chronic health issues may involve surgery, medications, or hospitalization.

- **Long-Term Care:** Senior dog accommodations, joint supplements, specialized diets, and increased veterinary visits.

Budgeting for these aspects ensures owners can provide a stable, healthy, and happy life for their Cavapoo without financial strain.

Ongoing Training and Socialization

Training and socialization are not limited to puppyhood; they are lifelong processes. Continuous reinforcement ensures a well-behaved, confident, and adaptable dog.

Ongoing Training Strategies:

- **Advanced Commands and Tricks:** Keep the mind engaged and strengthen the bond through learning new behaviors.
- **Socialization Updates:** Introduce new environments, people, and pets gradually to prevent fear or anxiety.

- **Behavioral Maintenance:** Address undesirable behaviors promptly using positive reinforcement and redirection.
- **Adaptation to Life Changes:** Reinforce training during moving, travel, or household adjustments to maintain consistency.

Health Monitoring and Aging Care

Lifelong health care is essential for sustaining a Cavapoo's quality of life. Proactive monitoring, preventive care, and adjustments in daily routines support longevity and comfort.

Key Aspects:

- **Regular Veterinary Checkups:** Annual exams for adults, biannual visits for seniors.
- **Vaccinations and Preventive Treatments:** Stay current with vaccines, flea/tick/heartworm preventives, and dental hygiene.
- **Dietary Adjustments:** Tailor nutrition for life stage, activity level, and health conditions.

- **Exercise Modifications:** Adjust intensity and duration based on mobility, joint health, and energy levels.
- **Monitoring for Age-Related Issues:** Observe for changes in behavior, appetite, mobility, or cognition, and consult the veterinarian as needed.

Coping with Health Challenges

Even with careful care, Cavapoos may encounter health challenges during their lifetime. Owners should approach these situations with knowledge, preparedness, and compassion.

Strategies for Effective Management:

- Maintain communication with your veterinarian for diagnosis, treatment options, and ongoing monitoring.
- Provide supportive care at home, including modifications to living spaces, mobility aids, or specialized feeding arrangements.
- Utilize mental stimulation, gentle play, and social interaction to maintain emotional well-being during illness.

- Make informed decisions regarding quality of life, balancing medical interventions with comfort and dignity.

Building a Lifelong Bond

The human-animal bond is central to responsible Cavapoo ownership. Emotional attachment, mutual trust, and shared experiences create a fulfilling relationship for both dog and owner.

Ways to Strengthen the Bond:

1. **Daily Interaction:** Consistent play, walks, training, and cuddling reinforce connection.
2. **Positive Reinforcement:** Encourage desirable behaviors through rewards and praise, fostering trust.
3. **Shared Experiences:** Travel, family activities, and special outings create memories and confidence.
4. **Recognition of Emotional Needs:** Respond to signs of stress, fear, or discomfort promptly to maintain emotional security.

5. **Celebration of Milestones:** Acknowledge birthdays, achievements in training, or recovery from illness to reinforce belonging and attachment.

Emotional Rewards of Ownership

Cavapoos provide more than companionship; they offer emotional enrichment that enhances human well-being:

- **Stress Reduction:** Interaction with dogs lowers cortisol and promotes relaxation.
- **Unconditional Love:** Cavapoos offer consistent affection and loyalty.
- **Social Support:** They can ease social interaction, particularly for children, seniors, or individuals living alone.
- **Purpose and Routine:** Caring for a dog instills responsibility, empathy, and structured daily living.
- **Joy and Entertainment:** Playfulness, curiosity, and unique personalities provide amusement and happiness.

Ethical and Community Considerations

Responsible Cavapoo ownership extends beyond the household:

- Advocate for hybrid dog welfare and responsible breeding practices.
- Encourage community awareness about Cavapoo needs, temperament, and socialization.
- Volunteer or engage in therapy, adoption awareness, or support for rescue organizations.
- Promote ethical treatment and discourage puppy mills or unregulated breeding practices.

Preparing for the Future

Responsible owners also consider long-term scenarios, including aging care, emergencies, or end-of-life planning:

- **Emergency Preparedness:** Maintain contacts for veterinarians, emergency clinics, and pet sitters.
- **Senior Care Planning:** Prepare for mobility aids, dietary changes, and increased veterinary visits.

- **Legacy Planning:** Consider arrangements for care in case of owner incapacity, such as trusted family members or legal pet guardianship.
- **Emotional Readiness:** Accept the finite nature of a dog's life while focusing on quality, enrichment, and shared experiences.

Summary

Owning a Cavapoo is a privilege that comes with profound responsibility. Lifelong commitment involves meeting physical, emotional, and social needs while planning for health challenges, financial responsibilities, and lifestyle adjustments. Ethical ownership requires thoughtful acquisition, consistent care, and ongoing enrichment, ensuring that the dog thrives as a valued family member.

By providing health care, training, socialization, mental stimulation, and love throughout the dog's life, owners not only safeguard well-being but also nurture the deep, rewarding bond that Cavapoos uniquely offer. The joy of owning a Cavapoo lies not only in companionship but in the shared journey of growth, learning, and mutual affection. Responsible ownership transforms the relationship into a lifelong partnership defined by trust, respect, and emotional fulfillment.

www.ingramcontent.com/pod-product-compliance
Lightning Source LLC
La Vergne TN
LVHW012357181125
825940LV00043B/1666